THE
ANOINTING

By

Judy Block

Published by:
Creative Press
P. O. Box 769000
Dallas, Texas 75376-9000

Copyright © 2014

ISBN# 978-0-89985-480-9

Scripture quotations noted NKJV are from THE NEW KING JAMES VERSION. © 1982 by Thomas Nelson, Inc. Used by permission. All rights reserved.

Scripture quotations taken from the NIV, and the Scripture quotations noted NIV are taken from the HOLY BIBLE, NEW INTERNATIONAL VERSION®. Copyright © 1973, 1978, 1984 by International Bible Society. Used by permission of Zondervan Bible Publishing House. All rights reserved.

Scripture quotations noted KJV are from The Holy Bible, KING JAMES VERSION.

Scripture quotations noted Amplified are from The Amplified Bible (AMP). The Old Testament copyright © 1965, 1987 by The Zondervan Corporation; New Testament, copyright © 1954, 1958, 1987 by The Lockman Foundation. Used by permission.

Vines Expository Dictionary of New Testament Words

Cover Design: Brandon Groomer

FOREWORD

It's Kingdom Time ... there's never been a time that we need the anointing of the Holy Spirit more than in this glorious End-Time Hour. I know the Lord is creating a deeper hunger and desire in the hearts of His people to have a greater understanding of the anointing of the Holy Spirit and how to move and live more effectively in the Spirit realm. Judy Block's book, *The Anointing* will be a great tool and asset to help many of us accomplish this. I believe this book and its message is right on time with God's end-time strategies and schedule.

R. A. Torrey once said ... "Before one can correctly understand the work of the Holy Spirit, he must first of all know the Spirit Himself." This book is not only replete with Scripture and revelation, personal experiences, and spiritual encounters, but the author bleeds through on every page with a sense of spiritual reality of her own personal relationship, respect and intimacy with the Holy Spirit. Judy knows the Holy Spirit of Whom she is writing and her heart's desire throughout this book is for you and others to come into an intimate spiritual relationship with Him, as well. So as you read, I know you will not only feel the heart of God drawing you, but you will also feel Judy's prayers and her heart's longing for you to know "The Anointing."

Dr. Jerry Howell

Pastor, Destiny Christian Center

TABLE OF CONTENTS

INTRODUCTION

Before you read this book I would like to pray for you.

Father God, I ask that when this person reads
this book, Your presence of the Holy Spirit's
Anointing would flood them and draw them
into a deeper relationship with you. I ask that
you give them revelation and new personal
insight of their friendship with the Holy Spirit
and His Anointing. Enlarge their hearts for
You, strengthen their stakes in Your Kingdom,
and cause them to increase and grow in You.
Touch them in a very real and meaningful way.
Thank you for being so good to us. I love You
and I am so thankful for You. In Jesus' Glorious
Name. Amen.

I've always enjoyed writing my personal revelations
from the Lord and have often wondered if He would ever
want me to do something with them. Needless to say He has
now.

When the Holy Spirit put it on my heart to write about
His Anointing and have it published, I purposely waited on

Him and tried to only write when He inspired me. It was difficult, being a housewife, mother, and on-call secretary for my husband. I had to work it in as I could, usually late at night and early in the morning, when everyone was sleeping.

Walking with Jesus in the power of His Anointing is vital to every believer. The real believers or remnant in these last days have got to have fellowship with the Holy Spirit and His powerful Anointing. The deception of the enemy is going to be so very great, you will need to be sensitive to the Holy Spirit to direct you to the real truth.

It is no mistake that you have picked up this book. Don't put it down. The enemy of your soul and your life does not want you to be set free. He does not want you to know the truth about the Holy Spirit. The revelation of having the infilling of the Holy Spirit is the most powerful thing that could ever happen to you. I know this is something the Lord wanted to give you. Take it, and live your life unashamedly full!

I am so thankful He gave me these wonderful truths, insights, and personal revelations about His Holy Spirit's Anointing. I know they were meant to be shared with you.

It is the truth that will set you free, not a compromise. Don't let someone keep you from receiving what God has for you, and don't compromise the amazing relationship you could have with God through His Holy Spirit.

Be blessed friend! Hopefully, one day we will meet.

Chapter 1

THE HOLY SPIRIT

The Anointing is the Holy Spirit. His presence, His power, and His Anointing, they are all one and the same. They are all Him.

If you want God's presence in your life, then you want the Holy Spirit. If you want God's power working in your life and on your behalf, then you want the Holy Spirit. And if you want the Anointing, then what you want is the Holy Spirit.

The Holy Spirit is just Who He says He is: Holy. He is not some weird spirit thing out there floating around. He is God the Father's presence with us. And since He is God's Holy presence, He cannot live in unholy vessels or people. Therefore, the Holy Spirit is reserved for living in God's children only. You must be purified by the blood of the Lamb, Jesus, for the atonement of your sins to be a child of God.

Now it is true, the Holy Spirit can come "upon" someone, but only by the direction of Jesus and His Heavenly Father, Jehovah God.

Example: 1 Samuel 10:1-11, Samuel anoints Saul as the king of Israel. (Emphasis added.)

"Samuel took a flask of olive oil and poured it over Saul's head. He kissed Saul on the cheek and said, 'I am doing this because the Lord has appointed you to be the leader of His people Israel ... At that time the Spirit of the Lord will come "upon" you in power (that is the manifested presence of God, His Holy Spirit) and you will prophesy with them ...'"

In the Old Testament, the Holy Spirit could only come "UPON" certain people. The authority Samuel had was to only tell Saul about the experience he was going to have. It was an experience for Saul to look forward to and to anticipate. It was not something Samuel could actually give to Saul. Samuel was not baptized in the Holy Spirit. The Holy Spirit was upon him and led him through an outer relationship, not from within.

In comparison, Jesus said in John 16:7, "Nevertheless I tell you the truth. It is to your advantage that I go away; for if I do not go away, the Helper will not come to you; but if I depart, I "will send" Him to you."

The English words, "come upon," in 1 Samuel is what we would look to in order to understand the receiving end of the "sent One." The words "come upon" mean simply "come to." However, when you look at the words in Hebrew, which Jesus said in John 16:7, you will notice there is a difference. The meaning of "will send" is "to thrust in!"

The words would have normally meant the same thing, but since it was Jesus speaking and not an Old Testament Prophet, the meaning of the words changed. They changed because of the authority of the One Who is speaking. The meaning of "will send" in Hebrew is "to thrust in!"

So what am I saying? In order to receive the "baptism" or total submersion or the "thrust into" of the Holy Spirit, you need Jesus and His eternal redemption.

> "But Christ came as High Priest of the good things to come, with the greater and more "perfect tabernacle" not made with hands, that is not of this creation. Not with the blood of goats and calves, but with His own blood He entered the Most Holy Place once for all, having obtained "eternal redemption." For if the blood of bulls and goats and the ashes of a heifer, sprinkling the unclean, sanctifies for the purifying of the flesh, how much more shall the blood of Christ (Jesus), who through the "eternal Spirit" offered Himself without spot to God, cleanse your conscience from dead

works to serve the living God? And for this reason He is the Mediator of the new covenant, by means of death, for the redemption of the transgressions under the first covenant, that those who are called may receive "the promise of the eternal inheritance." Hebrews 9:11-16.

On the day of Pentecost, the great outpouring of the promised Holy Spirit took place.

"Peter explained, 'Repent (turn away from doing evil), and be baptized (submerged totally) in the name of Jesus Christ for the remission (forgiveness) of sins; AND (then) you shall receive the gift (infilling, thrust into) of the Holy Spirit. For the promise is to you and to your children, and to all who are afar off, as many as the Lord our God will call.'" Acts 2:38-39.

It's a given. The Holy Spirit is Holy, and that is why He can only live in vessels that have been purified by the blood of Jesus.

You see, because of the blood of Jesus and His powerful resurrection, people who have accepted His sacrifice, have been imputed "thrust into" God's life and God's Spirit, making their dead spirits born again—born into God!

Yes, God the Father in Heaven, the creator of all life, has made a way for us to not only know Him, but to live with His very own Holy Spirit as our constant companion "in" us!

"Jesus said to Nicodemus, 'That which is born of the flesh is flesh, that which is born of the Spirit is spirit. Do not marvel that I said to you that you must be born again. The wind blows where it wishes, and you hear the sound of it, but cannot tell where it comes from or where it goes. So is everyone who is born of the Spirit.'" John 3:6-8.

It's a mystery. Jesus said,
"To you it has been given to know the mystery of the Kingdom of God, but to those who are outside, all things come in parables." Mark 4:11.

So don't even try to explain it to the people of the world. They will not understand it, and they will argue with you, for unless they are born-again, unless their spirit-man becomes alive by the powerful life giving blood of Jesus, it is absolute foolishness to them. In order to understand Spiritual things, you must be a Spiritual person.

"Those who are dominated by their sinful nature (who live according to the flesh) think about sinful things, (They set their minds on the things of the flesh: what they want.), but those who are controlled by the Holy Spirit think about things that please the Spirit (that is God). If your sinful nature controls your mind, (If you are carnally minded), there is death. (But to be Spiritually minded), if the Holy Spirit controls your mind, there is life and peace. For the sinful nature is always hostile (against) God. (Immediately, your sinful nature rises up and wants to do what he wants to do. He wants to be in control. He, your sinful nature, does not want what God has for you. It naturally goes the wrong way.) It never did obey God's law (His way of doing things), and it never will. That is why those who are still under the control of their sinful nature (the flesh) can never please God."

Romans 8:5-8 (AMP). (Emphasis added.)

So, how can your spirit-man become born again? What is this mystery? The mystery is: your spirit is like a seed.

You have your body, which is your physical body.

You have your soul, which is your mind, your will, and your emotions. And you have your spirit, which is like a seed of faith waiting to come to life.

Your spirit-man's seed is "faith." Your seed has a name. It's your name and faith. For example: My name is Judy Ann. So my seed's name is "Judy Ann Faith." It's who you are. Your name is your seed, and inside your seed is faith. Your faith is waiting. Your seed is waiting. "Bubba Joe's Faith" is waiting!

The seed has the potential to be great, but can do nothing on its own. The seed must become alive. Your name's faith must come to life. It needs to break out of its hard shell to grow, and it does that by dying to itself and opening its heart to the love of God. Then the love of God will cause your name's faith to spring into life. The love of God, what Jesus did for you, will bring life to you.

When you want Him, when you call upon the Name of the Lord, you will become born again.

> "But someone would ask, 'How will the dead be raised? (How can your spirit-man come to life?!) What kind of bodies will they have? (What kind of body does a born-again spirit have?)' What a foolish question! When you plant a seed into the ground, it doesn't grow into a plant unless it dies first. And what you

put in the ground is not the plant that will grow, but only a dry little seed of wheat or whatever it is that you are planting. THEN GOD GIVES IT A NEW BODY, JUST THE KIND HE WANTS IT TO HAVE. A different kind of plant grows from each kind of seed!'"
1 Corinthian 15:35-38. (Emphasis added.)

"A DIFFERENT KIND OF PLANT GROWS FROM EACH KIND OF SEED!"

God will give your spirit-man a body! You will become born of the Spirit! It's a mystery! You cannot see Him, but He is there.

Your spirit-man will grow into the man God has intended for you. You see, the purpose, the plans, the calling and the destiny, these are things God has in His heart for you, and they are really for you! He wants to help you and bless you in your life's journey.

"For God so loved the world that He gave His only begotten Son, that whoever believes in Him should not perish but have everlasting (eternal) life." John 3:16.

Jesus was the only begotten Son of God. He was and is God's gift to us for eternal life. He was the only One Who could go in our place and bring us back to God the Father. Jesus was the only one who could and was born without sin. He was not born of a man's seed. He was born of a virgin, placed in her womb by the Holy Spirit. That is what makes it such a great miracle from God.

Jesus was already the Lord of Glory, the Son of God, before He was born in His earthman suit. He was with God the Father before time even began, which also means He was with God the Father during His creation of life. As a matter of fact, they made everything together. Here are the Scriptures to prove it, Genesis 1:26, John 1:1-3, and John 3:12-13.

Everyone in the world was born into the sin of Adam, already smudged by the state of fallen man, the soul alive, yet the spirit man dead, separated from God. (Romans 5:12-17; 1 Corinthians 15:21-22, 45). But, because Jesus lived a spotless, sinless life, He was able to be the sacrifice for our sin, and die in our place. He was the only One Who could do it.

"When Adam sinned, sin entered the entire human race. Adam's sin brought death, so death spread to everyone, for everyone was born into sin. Yes, people sinned even before the law was given. And though there was no law to break, since it had not yet been given, they all died anyway, even though they did not disobey an explicit commandment of God, as Adam did. What a contrast between Adam and Christ, who was yet to come. And what a difference between our sin and God's generous gift of forgiveness. For this one man, Adam, brought death to many through his sin. But this other man, Jesus Christ, brought forgiveness to many through God's bountiful gift. And the result of God's gracious gift is very different from the result of that one man's sin. For Adam's sin led to condemnation, but we have the free gift of being accepted by God, even though we are guilty of many sins. The sin of this one man, Adam, caused death to rule over us, but all who receive God's wonderful, gracious gift of righteousness will live in triumph over sin and death through this one man, Jesus Christ." Romans 5:12-17.

Death is separation from God. Life is being alive in God. Jesus lived a life, without the fallen state of sin in Him, which means He had no death in Him. He was totally alive when the Holy Spirit placed Him in a virgin's womb, and lived His life on the Earth totally alive with no sin.

So when Jesus died on the cross, He took our sins upon Himself as our sacrifice. After He died, and went to Hell, on the third day the Holy Spirit raised Him from the dead. At that point the Scriptures say He made an open display of the devil, and took back the keys to death and hell. This is what gives us the victory again to not have to live under the curse of the law of sin and death, which came from Adam's original sin. Jesus' blood paid the price for us to be free. He bought us back and broke the bondage of death over our lives. Alleluia!

Thus, giving us the ability to become born-again, alive in God!

The mystery: When you asked Jesus to forgive you of your sins, He took the key of death and broke the lock off your heart, your seed's faith, and gave you life! Thus "your name faith," your seed of faith, became alive, became born-again! You became a new living creature, alive unto God, and dead to sin! (2 Corinthians 5:15-19).

> "O death, where is your sting?! O Hades, where is your victory?! The sting of death is sin, and the strength of sin is the law. But thanks be to God who gives us the victory through our Lord Jesus Christ!" 1 Corinthians 15:55-56.

WHY YOU NEED THE HOLY SPIRIT

Ah! But there is still more! It, meaning your spirit-man, "your name Faith," will only live for so long on its own. Here's the mystery again: "The wind blows where it wishes, and you hear the sound of it, but cannot tell where it comes from or where it goes. So is everyone who is born of the Spirit."

To the world, or those who do NOT know Him, the wind of the Spirit is foolishness. It doesn't make any sense to them. It's just wind blowing with no direction ... a pipe dream. As well, Spirit-led people are foolishness to them.

It is the wind of the Spirit Who brings revelation to those who are open to receive. Jesus said I will send the Helper to you. Or you could say it like this, "I will 'thrust into' you the Helper!" What does He help you with? Everything!

Your spirit-man will only live for so long without the relationship of the Holy Spirit, which is the care and leadership of the Holy Spirit. It's like a plant without water. It will die.

Without the Holy Spirit watering (feeding) your spirit-man, you are operating on soul power! Without the fellowship of the Anointing oil of the Holy Spirit to lubricate your life, (to minister to your life), you are operating on soul power, even if you are born-again.

You do not want to do that! This is what is called a carnal Christian: One who tries to live and serve God in their own strength and abilities, putting their trust in mankind or a religion, instead of Him. It is the most difficult and frustrating thing anyone could try to do, because without the relationship of the Holy Spirit, it is impossible.

There are those who would prefer to follow a man or a cause, rather than to know the truth. But I believe you are not that person! You are reading this book because you are hungry for the truth!

Jesus said the Holy Spirit will lead you to all truth! Let Him! If Jesus said He is the way the truth and the life, then you have no worries. The Holy Spirit will always lead you to Jesus. He will never contradict His word.

Many would say, "But it is the watering of the word that causes you to grow." Yes! That is exactly right! What is the water that brings revelation to the word?! The Holy Spirit's Anointing!

When you are a born-again believer, as you read the Word, the Bible, it's the Holy Spirit Who breaths life on it. He brings revelation of the Word and how it applies to you. He is the Anointing Who brings God's manifested power into your life.

When the Holy Spirit is living on the inside of someone, there is "good fruit" that abounds. There is an ability to follow God's leading. There is an ability to say "no" to the flesh and "yes" to His will.

God not only provided a way to become born again through what Jesus did for us, but He also provided a way for us to live in constant fellowship with Him through the Holy Spirit. Wow! He is so awesome!

You see, God is not magic. He is real. He does not do anything by magic. Magic is deceptive, just like the devil. Magic would lead you to believe something, but it is really a lie. The devil would like for you to believe that God is the same way; He is deceptive like magic. He would like for you to believe that God does not do what you think He should do, because He is not real. But that is a lie from the devil who hates you. And the devil is not only THE LIAR, but he will deceive you, if you let him!

God is real! What God does in your life is eternal. It is real! He really works today and does great things on the Earth. But He works through His Holy Spirit and through His born-again, Spirit-filled people.

There is nothing deceptive about God except to the devil. God is smart and keeps things cloaked from the devil because the devil is evil, just like his name, D-evil, or the evil one.

There is something you need to realize. God the Father is in Heaven. He has provided a way for you to get to know Him through His Son, Jesus, and by His baptism in His Holy Spirit He has provided a way for you to be in constant fellowship with Him.

There is nothing weird about the Holy Spirit. He is God's presence here on the Earth today.

Is God weird? I don't think so!

Are you weird? Maybe! Without God, we are all

missing it, but with God, we are all being led by His perfectness working in and through us.

> "Then Peter said to them, (1) Repent (turn away from doing evil), (2) and be baptized (submerged in water) in the name of Jesus Christ for the remission (forgiveness) of sins; (3) and you shall receive the gift (the "thrust into," the infilling) of the Holy Spirit. For the promise (this covenant with God) is to you and to your children, and to all who are afar off, as many as the Lord our God will call."
> Acts 2:38-39. (Emphasis added.)

Now this is a real problem for many Christians today. They believe that because they are born-again, they already have the Holy Spirit. What they have is the imputed power of the blood of Jesus that caused their spirit-man to be washed clean of sin, and thus become born-again.

Jesus is the key to eternal life!

This is worth repeating. The powerful blood of Jesus when applied to your spirit-man's seed, breaks the lock of death off of you and causes your spirit-man to come to life!

Now, the Holy Spirit is with those people who don't believe in the baptism of the Holy Spirit, and He is trying to help them, but He CANNOT help them in the capacity He wants to. He can only do what they allow Him to do, because there is no inner-man fellowship. The inner-man fellowship and friendship of the Holy Spirit is the key to growing in the spirit! It is impossible to do so without Him.

> "For 'They profess to know God, but in works deny Him, being abominable, disobedient, and disqualified for every good work.'" Titus 1:16.

Disqualified! You've got to have the baptism of the Holy Spirit! You don't want to confess you have Him and find out later you never knew Him!

Remember, the Holy Spirit can come UPON you and do great things through you, but the baptism of the Holy Spirit is the total submersion of the Holy Spirit's life living IN you. This is where the fellowship and friendship of the Holy Spirit grows. "In you!"

The Old Testament prophets did not deny Him. The Holy Spirit came upon them and had fellowship with them, but from the outside in. Today, because of Jesus, we can have the fellowship of the Holy Spirit from the inside out.

Our example is Jesus. Jesus was God incarnate. Yet, He needed the baptism of the Holy Spirit! He did nothing on His own. It was after He received the baptism of the Holy Spirit that He did all of His miracles. Jesus not only needed, but wanted the friendship, and the Anointing of the Holy

Spirit. If Jesus, the Son of God, needed the baptism of the Holy Spirit, how much more do we?!

The disciples were believers. They were born again. Yet, they needed the baptism of the Holy Spirit. They needed the Anointing. It was after they were filled with the Holy Spirit's Anointing that over 3,000 people were saved in one day! Only God's manifested presence through the Holy Spirit's Anointing could do such a thing!

Even Paul had the baptism. He believed Jesus was the Son of God. He was born again, and yet, he said that he spoke in tongues more than anyone else! (1 Corinthians 14:18). He needed to write "in" the inspiration and Anointing of the Holy Spirit. Where do you think he got all his revelation?! Yes! He got it from the constant companionship of the Holy Spirit!

The disciples were baptizing people in the Holy Spirit on a daily basis. So it wasn't just for the disciples!

People in the New Testament believed in Jesus as their Savior, and then they were baptized with the fellowship of the Holy Spirit, not just with water. Acts 9:17-18; Acts 10:44-48; Acts 11:15-18; Acts 15:6-9; Acts 19:1-6. Over and over again, you can read about it.

It was not just a 50 or 100 year span of time and then the Holy Spirit ran out, as if there was no more left for the rest of us. Do you think God will run out or be used up like a glass of water? No, that's not possible! And that's what makes Him so wonderful, His water, His presence, His Holy Spirit never runs out! He never runs dry! The Living Water of His Holy Presence never stops flowing! How wonderful! He's the same yesterday, today and forever. (Hebrews 13:8). His mercies are new every morning, and His baptism is just as much for us today as He was for the disciples back then.

The Holy Spirit has been baptizing people now for over 2,000 years! Today, you CANNOT rule out the baptism of the Holy Spirit. We need Him as much as they did in the days of the New Testament.

Jesus said that in the last days it was going to be so difficult that He would shorten the days to His return, because even the elect would not be able to make it. Does that sound like we need the baptism of the Holy Spirit and His anointing?! It certainly does! He wasn't just talking about then. He was talking about now! We are living in the last days!

There is no doubt, the Holy Spirit lives on the Earth today. There is no doubt people are being baptized in His powerful presence and friendship every day.

Don't limit yourself. Be open-minded to what God has for you. He is so awesome! He is NOT going to do something weird to you. He is going to fill you with His Spirit, His manifested Presence!

There is more to this walk with God than just being born-again, that is just the start of your journey with God. There is even more to this walk with God than His written Word, the Bible. It is the manifested presence and fellowship of the Holy Spirit! It works together: salvation through Jesus, and the infilling of the Holy Spirit. He brings it all to the table for you.

Jesus not only died for our sins, but afterwards He rose from the dead, He ascended to Heaven, so we could have the Holy Spirit. He wanted us to have the Holy Spirit, His fellowship, His friendship and His Anointing.

Jesus said to His disciples the night He was betrayed that He would not leave us without help.

> "Nevertheless I tell you the truth. It is to your advantage that I go away; for if I do not go away, the Helper (the Holy Spirit) will not come to you; but if I depart, I will send Him to you." John 16:7.

> "But when the Helper (the Holy Spirit) comes, whom I will send to you from the Father, the Spirit of Truth, who proceeds from the Father, He will testify of Me." John 17:26.

After He was crucified, He spent three days taking the keys of death, hell and the grave away from the devil. Then when He was raised from the dead, He spent 40 days with His disciples, and many other people to prove Who He was and what He had done.

"And being assembled together with them, He (Jesus) commanded them not to depart from Jerusalem, but to wait for the Promise of the Father, "which" He said, 'you have heard from Me; for John truly baptized with water, but you shall be baptized with the HOLY SPIRIT not many days from now.' Therefore, when they had come together, they asked Him, saying, 'Lord, will you at this time restore the Kingdom to Israel?' And He said to them, 'It is not for you to know times or seasons which the Father has put in His own authority. BUT YOU SHALL RECEIVE POWER WHEN THE HOLY SPIRIT HAS COME UPON (THRUST INTO) YOU; and you shall be witnesses to Me in Jerusalem, and in all Judea and Samaria, and to the end of the earth.' Now when He had spoken these things, while they watched, He was taken up, and a cloud received Him out of their sight." Acts 1:4-9.

Jesus was then taken up to Heaven, received His new Crown of Glory, and sat down at the right hand of His Father, God Almighty, the Great and All Powerful, One and Only True Living God!

"My dear children, I write this to you so that you will not sin. But if anybody does sin, we have one who speaks to the Father in our defense—Jesus Christ, the Righteous One. He is the atoning sacrifice for our sins, and not only for ours but also for the sins of the whole world." 1 John 2:1-2 (NIV).

God the Father is in Heaven. Jesus is in Heaven, sitting at the right hand of the Father, talking to Him and interceding for us on our behalf. The Holy Spirit is God's presence here on the Earth for us.

SPEAKING IN TONGUES

"And when the day of Pentecost was fully come, they were all with one accord in one place. And suddenly there came a sound from Heaven, as of a rushing mighty wind, and it filled the whole house where they were sitting. Then there appeared to them divided tongues, as of fire, and one sat upon each of them. And they were all filled with the Holy Spirit and began to speak with other tongues, as the Spirit gave them utterance." Acts 2:1-4.

There are no if, ands, or buts about it. The evidence that you have received the infilling of the Holy Spirit is speaking in tongues.

"Jesus said, 'These signs shall follow them that believe ... they shall speak with new tongues.'"
Mark 16:17.

Here are some other Scriptures that speak about the gift of speaking in tongues as a result of the baptism of the Holy Spirit—Acts 2:11; Acts 10:44-47; Acts 19:1-7.

I can personally say the baptism of the Holy Spirit is for today, because I have received the Holy Spirit and His Anointing through His baptism, and I immediately received my prayer language by speaking in tongues. My personal experience with the baptism of the Holy Spirit was a separate experience than when I was born again. Yet, my husband's experience was all at one time, he immediately received his prayer language when he got saved. It was an outward manifestation of something that had happened on the inside. The Holy Spirit filled him to overflowing with His presence and love! He didn't even know what had happened! It was a supernatural experience, because God is supernatural!

When I received the Holy Spirit, it was soft, sweet and precious. But when I spoke in tongues, it also was an overflow of God's presence and love.

It's true that the outward manifestation of the baptism of the Holy Spirit is speaking in other languages or as the Bible says, tongues. I personally know many people who have the baptism of the Holy Spirit with speaking in other tongues. There are hundreds of thousands of people today, living all over this Earth, who have the baptism of the Holy Spirit and speak in tongues. You cannot deny this fact. There must be something to it.

However, there are those who believe they have the baptism without the evidence of speaking in tongues. I hope I don't offend you, but the Bible is very clear, and from my own personal experience, I believe that the evidence of the infilling of the Holy Spirit is the gift of speaking in tongues. It's a powerful way of knowing, without a doubt, that you have received the Holy Spirit baptism. It is a powerful gift for you!

If you are not personally sure, if you have the baptism or not, then you probably don't. That is why receiving the gift of tongues is so important. Because when you get filled, and you speak in tongues, something is different, and you know it! It's natural to question if you've got it or not, but when you speak in tongues, there is that stamp on it that says, "You got it."

However, I believe there is another real way to know. Ask yourself these questions:

- Do you have a relationship with the Holy Spirit?
- Do you feel and know His presence?
- Do you spend time with Him in your secret place?
- Does He daily breathe revelation on the Word for you?
- Have you consistently felt His power, revelation and prophetic flow in prayer?
- Do you know His voice?
- Are you growing?
- Does He speak to you on a regular basis?

These are real questions to ask yourself because this is the lifestyle of Spirit-filled people.

I know this sounds like I might be contradicting myself, but I'm not. I really want you to think about this. Every time you receive something special from the Lord, especially when you first start walking with Him, the enemy will try to steal it away from you. The devil and his followers do not want you Spirit-filled. He does not want you to know who you are in Jesus or know your place of authority.

When you receive the baptism of the Holy Spirit, the devil will try to convince you there's a reason why you didn't receive. He will lie to you and tell you all kinds of awful stuff about you, but as long as you know you are under attack, you can overcome those lies. He does not want you to get the baptism of the Holy Spirit. He hates you, and he hates God. He wants to destroy you and try to make you doubt it could or did ever happen to you.

That's why your prayer language is so important. He cannot fight against your prayer language, because it is the Holy Spirit!

Here's the real truth. If you already have the baptism of the Holy Spirit, then you have a real and meaningful relationship with Him. If you do not have that, then you probably don't have the Holy Spirit. That is what the baptism of the Holy Spirit is all about. It's about living this life with the constant companionship of the Holy Spirit. He's not only your best friend, but He is everything to you.

That is why the outward manifestation of the gift of the Holy Spirit is speaking in tongues, and it's for you!

I know a lot of people think it is only supposed to be used as a sign to the lost. Really? The All-Wise, All-Knowing, Creator of All-Life is going to use the gift of tongues for one reason? That doesn't sound right, because it's not!

It's a sign for you, too, and even more than that.

Jude, the half brother of Jesus, wrote the letter of Jude to the readers to stir up the gift of the Holy Spirit's Anointing through their prayer language. He wanted to appeal to them to contend for their faith in Jesus by praying in the Spirit, with their gift of tongues! Why? Because when you pray in your prayer language, your faith and spirit-man is strengthened, encouraged, and inspired. It's God's Holy Spirit speaking through you!

> "But you, dear friends, must continue to build your lives on the foundation of your Holy faith. And continue to pray as you are directed by the Holy Spirit." Jude 17 (NLT).

> "But you, dear friends, must build up your lives ever more strongly upon the foundation of our Holy faith, learning to pray in the power and strength of the Holy Spirit." Jude 17 (TLB).

It's true; praying in the Spirit builds up and strengthens your spirit-man. That's why it is so important to have the gift of tongues. You really need the insight and revelation that comes by praying in the Holy Ghost.

Paul wrote: "I thank God! That I speak in (strange) tongues (languages) more than any of you or all of you put together!" (Emphasis added).

Paul wasn't speaking in tongues just for the lost, or just to interpret for others. Paul spoke in tongues, gratefully and fanatically! Why? Because it made him strong in the ways of the Holy Spirit! It was causing him to grow in the Spirit. His spirit-man was being watered, nurtured, strengthened and was growing in revelation through the baptism of the Holy Spirit!

When you speak in tongues, you have tapped into the person of the Holy Spirit's Anointing. The Holy Spirit's Anointing is God's supernatural manifested power!

That is why I said, do not limit yourself. The baptism, which is the indwelling fellowship of the Holy Spirit, is for anyone who wants Him. The only criteria is that you must be born again.

RECEIVE THE HOLY SPIRIT

The baptism of the Holy Spirit is for you! He wants to help you and anoint you with His awesome presence inside and out. He is the power of the resurrection. He is the power you need to walk with God on this Earth and in this life.

He is revelation! He gives insight to the things you need to know about. He is the One Who will lead you and guide you and help you make decisions. He is everything you need to make it in this life. And He is so awesome!

Now you ask me, "How do I receive the baptism of the Holy Spirit?"

Pursue Him! I am going to tell you to pursue Him with all your heart and everything you've got.

For most people, getting born again meant finding yourself at the end of your rope, desperate for help. They had to pursue God with all their heart. And then there are others who simply believed and they got born again and baptized.

It's time for a real and meaningful change! If you want more of God, this is the only way to get it!

> "He is a rewarder of those who earnestly and diligently seek Him!" Hebrews 11:6b (NIV).

How it will happen for you? I do not know. But I do know the Holy Spirit wants you to really want Him. Who doesn't want to be wanted? Who doesn't want to be loved? Who doesn't want to be pursued?

He is the prize!

He is worth pursuing!

God has so much invested in you. Yes you! He created the Earth and all the wonderful life here for you. He created the Heavens and all that goes on out there for you. He sent His only Son to die a cruel death for the punishment of your sins. He raised Jesus from the dead, and it is recorded that Jesus stayed on the Earth for 40 days as a witness to the people that He was raised from the dead for them and for you. He sent His Holy Spirit for you. He's allowed men to give their lives to make available His Holy Scriptures for you. And there is so much more He has done just for you! Yes, He has a lot invested in you. His life! All that He is, and all that He has!

The baptism of the Holy Spirit is God's gift to you. He wants to help you. He wants to be your best friend.

"He is a friend who is closer than a brother."
Proverbs 18:24.

The Holy Spirit loves you and is drawing you to Himself, but you have to want Him, and pursue Him, too.

In Matthew 7:7-11, Jesus said,
"Ask, and it will be given to you;
Seek, and you will find;
Knock, and it will be opened to you.
For everyone who asks receives,
And he who seeks finds,
And to him who knocks it will be opened.
"Or what man is there among you who, if his son   asks for bread, will give him a stone? Or if he asks for a fish, will give him a serpent? If you then, being evil, know how to give good gifts to your children, how much the more will your Father who is in Heaven give good things to those who ask Him!"

Prayer:

Lord, I lift up to You this person who is searching and looking for You, for more of You. I pray You would reveal Yourself to them in a new and real way. I pray You would grant them the cry of their heart, to know you more. Holy Spirit Anointing, fall fresh upon them and reveal Yourself to them. Fill them and submerge them with Your baptism, Your indwelling. Give them Your Anointing and the Gifts of the Spirit. Show them your ways and guide them to Your truth in personal revelation. Thank you for being so good to us. In Jesus' Glorious Name I pray, Amen.

I would like to say one more thing to you about the baptism of the Holy Spirit. When you do receive Him, and you will, don't stop pursuing Him. They call it practicing His presence, which simply means spending time with Him alone in His presence. Allow Him to help you grow. Follow His leading. He loves you.

Chapter 2

OUR PLACE OF AUTHORITY

One night, sometime in the fall of 2008, about 2 a.m., I suddenly woke up. It is a habit for me to go and pray, if I wake up in the middle of the night. You never know what is going on, and you need be attentive to the leading of the Holy Spirit.

I didn't want to wake up my husband, so I quietly got up and went into the formal living room. I was more than just tired. I felt I had been awakened from a deep sleep. It was very difficult, but I was trying to pray and be attentive.

Finally, I decided there wasn't anything going on, so I started to wonder if there was anyone else, besides me, who actually got up in the middle of the night to pray. I was kind of complaining to myself about it, and quietly said to the Holy Spirit, jokingly, "Well, I guess I'm just a different breed." And when I said that, I immediately had a vision.

THE VISION

I was riding on a white horse along side of the Lord Jesus, Who was also riding on a white horse. There were thousands of others as far as the eye could see, who were also riding along side and behind us on white horses. We were all dressed in "white uniform-like for battle" clothes; none were exactly alike, absolutely beautiful and immaculate, and so were the horses; they were amazing. We were coming down out of the sky on our way to what seemed to be a great battle, and the Lord was leading the way.

THE INTERPRETATION

I can't say the Holy Spirit spoke to me. It was an overall knowing, all at once, when He dropped the interpretation of the dream in me.

"My horse, the one I was riding on, is my place of Authority in Him. My place of Authority is my Anointing. My Anointing is what I am gifted in. And my gift is the call on my life."

My vision is scriptural. It is found in Revelation 19:11-16 (NIV).

"Now I saw Heaven standing open and there before me was a white horse, whose rider is called Faithful and True. With justice He judges and makes war. His eyes are like blazing fire, and on His head are many crowns. He has a name written on Him that no one knows but Himself. He is dressed in a robe dipped in blood, and His name is the Word of God. The armies of heaven were following Him, riding on white horses and dressed in fine linen, white and clean. Out of His mouth comes a sharp sword with which to strike down the nations. 'He will rule them with an iron scepter.' He treads the winepress of the fury of the wrath of God Almighty. On His robe and on His thigh He has this name written: KING OF KINGS AND LORD OF LORDS."

Wow! So, what are we talking about? The Anointing! What is the Anointing? It is the tangible manifested presence of the Holy Spirit.

What is "your" Anointing? "Your personal Anointing" is the manifested presence of the Holy Spirit on "your" very own personal gifts and calling.

In my personal walk with the Lord, I have found there are established definite times when the Holy Spirit's Anointing will flow or manifest Himself.

1. He flows in your secret place of prayer, where you commune and spend time with Him alone. (Matthew 6:6; 1 John 2:27).
2. He flows in your gifts and calling. (Romans 11:29, 12:3-8).
3. He flows where there are two or more believers in unity. (Matthew 18:19; Psalm 133:1-3).
4. He flows where He is welcomed.

Now you know you can't put God in a box. He is so awesome, and He really does love to show up wherever He is welcomed. I'm sure there are other times and reasons the Holy Spirit's Anointing will manifest, but I've found these four to be the main ones.

Now, according to this vision I had, your place of Authority is the Anointing. Is that scriptural? Absolutely, it is!

Our example is our Lord and Savior, Jesus. He was a man of the ultimate, great Authority in the ultimate, great Anointing. But was it simply because He was the Son of God on the Earth? No. You see, nothing can ever change the fact that Jesus is the Son of God. However, when He came to the Earth, He emptied Himself of all His Heavenly glory as the Son of God and Co-Creator with God to become the Son of Man. That amazing fact is what makes Him so wonderful and spectacular! Jesus had to live His whole life of 30 years, before His baptism, without sin and with no help from anyone as the Son of Man. He was still God the Father's Son, nothing could ever change that, but without all the glory and power He had as the Son of God and as Co-Creator with God.

"Let this mind be in you which was also in Christ Jesus, who, being in the form of God (God's Son), did not consider it robbery to be equal with God (Co-Creator), but made Himself of no reputation (He left everything He was in Heaven as the Son of God and Co-Creator with God), taking the form of a bondservant (He became God the Father's servant, or considered Himself to be God's slave instead of His son), and coming in the likeness of men (He came to the earth to be like a man). And being found in appearance as a man, He humbled Himself and became obedient to the point of death, (He refused to think highly of Himself as the Son of God even as the Co-Creator with God and humbled Himself to be like a mere man, His own creation) and became obedient to the point of death, (He laid everything down to the point of death) even the death of the cross." Philippians 2:5-8, (Emphasis added).

I love how the Amplified Version says it:

"Let this same attitude and purpose and (humble) mind be in you which was in Christ Jesus; (Let Him be your example in humility) Who, although being essentially one with God and in the form of God (possessing the fullness of the attributes which make God, God), did not think this equality with God was a thing to be eagerly grasped or retained, But stripped Himself (of all privileges and rightful dignity), so as to assume the guise of a servant (slave), in that He became like men and was born a human being. And after He had appeared in human form, He abased and humbled Himself (still further) and CARRIED HIS OBEDIENCE to the extreme of death, even the death of the cross!"

That is so powerful! The one and only Son of God laid down His life totally and completely for us!

Now don't forget, we are talking about the authority we have in the Anointing!

Let's read a little further in the Amplified Version in Philippians 2, starting where we left off in verse 11.

"Therefore (because He (Jesus) stooped so low) God has highly exalted Him and has freely bestowed on Him the name that is above every name, That in (at) the name of Jesus every knee should (must) bow, in Heaven and on Earth and under the earth, And every tongue (frankly and openly) confess and acknowledge that Jesus Christ is Lord, to the glory of God the Father.

So then, this great Authority and this great Anointing that Jesus had, came with a great price.

THE SEAL OF APPROVAL

"Then Jesus came from Galilee to John at the Jordan to be baptized by him … When He had been baptized, Jesus came up immediately from the water, and behold, the Heavens were opened to Him, and he (John) saw the Spirit of God (the Holy Spirit) descending like a dove and alighting upon (Jesus). And suddenly a voice came from Heaven saying, 'This is My beloved Son, in whom I am well pleased.'" Matthew 3:13, 16-17; 4:1-3a.

Immediately, when Jesus came up out of the water from being baptized, the Holy Spirit came upon Him in the form of a dove. The Holy Spirit is not a bird. He had the appearance of a dove. It was a sign for all to see. The Holy Spirit's Anointing filled Jesus in His baptism. It was the baptism of the Holy Spirit.

God does everything for a purpose and is perfect in everything He does. Jesus received the Holy Spirit right when He was being baptized in water, so we could see that the Holy Spirit is a baptism. When you are baptized in the Holy Spirit you are submerged in Him, totally like water baptism.

And then a voice from Heaven spoke. It was God the Father, and He said, "This is My beloved Son, in whom I am well pleased."

What just happened? First of all the Holy Spirit came upon Jesus in that very special way, so that everyone could see and testify to what had happened.

Everyone there saw it with their very own eyes. They saw the Holy Spirit come upon Him in the appearance of a dove. Everyone there heard God's audible voice speak and testify He was God's Son! And even though it doesn't say it, I bet they could all feel the power of that moment, too!

Just think, the manifested presence of the Holy Spirit in full strength on and in the Son of Man! There were probably waves of His love illuminating from Him!

What a powerful, powerful moment!

When God the Father spoke, "This is My beloved Son in whom I am well pleased," He gave Jesus His Seal of Approval! God approved of Jesus. He was well pleased with His Son, Who had lived a sinless life and had given Himself to His Heavenly Father's will, all on His own for 30 years.

Jesus, the Son of Man, did it all on His own. He lived a sinless life without any help from anyone. He was God as man for us. He was our redeemer. He did what we could not do. And He was our perpetuation, which means it was done one time for all and for all eternity.

The gift of the Holy Spirit was God the Father's Seal of Approval given to Jesus. This Seal of Approval is His Authority on Earth as it is in Heaven!

> "And Jesus came and spoke to them (the disciples), saying, 'All Authority has been given to Me in Heaven and on Earth.'"
> Matthew 28:18.

If all Authority had been given to Him, that means it was a gift! What was the gift? It was God the Father's baptism in the Holy Spirit!

Has He not done the same with us? When we believe in Jesus as our Savior, what does Jesus do? He gives us His Seal of Approval with the gift of the baptism of the Holy Spirit.

Only in Jesus could we possibly have been given Authority. Only in Jesus could we possibly receive the gift of the Holy Spirit, which means you must be born of the Spirit through Jesus. That is why receiving the Holy Spirit is a separate gift. It is a gift from Jesus to those of us who believe in Him and WHO WANT HIM!

Why do people fight so hard to believe the Holy Spirit is for today and for them?! Because it is the Authority God Almighty has given to us through Jesus! The devil and the world do not want you to know your Authority! Nor does he want you live in it through the power of the awesome presence of the Anointing and the fellowship of the Holy Spirit!

There is the gift of salvation when we receive the forgiveness of our sins and our spirit-man becomes alive in God. Then there is the gift of the baptism of the Holy Spirit. It is God's gift of Authority for us through Jesus.

It is the manifested presence of the Holy Spirit's Anointing that causes things to happen. Without Him we can do nothing.

Your Anointing is the gift of the Holy Spirit on your personal gifts, talents, and abilities He has given to you. Those gifts, talents, and abilities are what make you the unique person you are. You have Authority in your gifts, talents, and abilities through the gift of the Holy Spirit which is Jesus' favor and approval of you. He approves of you! He loves you! He wants to bless you and help you!

"And (Jesus) said to them, 'I saw Satan, fall like lightning from Heaven. BEHOLD, I GIVE YOU THE AUTHORITY!!! Nevertheless do not rejoice in this, that the spirits are subject to you, but rather rejoice because your names are written in Heaven." Luke 10:18-20.

Jesus said to us, "BEHOLD, I GIVE YOU AUTHORITY!"

"Jesus approached and, breaking the silence, said to them, ALL AUTHORITY (THAT IS ALL POWER OF RULERSHIP) in Heaven and on Earth has been given to Me. Go then ..." Matthew 28:18 (AMP).

And then He tells His disciples what He wants them to do with His Authority, and with His power of Rulership that He has given to them.

Jesus would not send His disciples to do His work without the ability to do it. So He did. He equipped them and allowed the Holy Spirit to go with them in the power of His Rulership, His Authority, and His Anointing. This was before the Cross. So He sent the Holy Spirit with them. They did not receive the baptism yet, not until the day of Pentecost.

And just like Jesus our Savior, we have been given a more

excellent way through the baptism of the Holy Spirit. He has given us His Seal of Approval. He has given us His Authority, His power of Rulership, His Anointing, His very present help and friendship! Now we are equipped to do His work and live this life in humble victory! I say humble, because it is all Jesus and the Holy Spirit's empowerment that gives us the victory.

So, let me tell you straight up, with your gift of Authority is the Anointing and the Anointing is the Holy Spirit. So then, just like Jesus, your gift of Authority is the BAPTISM of the Holy Spirit!

Do you want the rightful gift of Authority Jesus has purchased for you? Then you want the gift of the baptism of the Holy Spirit!

JESUS KNEW WHO HE WAS

Jesus knew He was the Co-Creator with God the Father when He was on the Earth as the Son of Man. He knew His creation. He was a vital part of it all when it happened, and I believe, He was not born without the memory of where He had come from or Who He was. I believe He remembered it all when He was on the Earth. After all, He was the perfect Son of Man, God incarnate.

I think of the time He cursed the fig tree, and it shriveled up and died. (Matthew 21:18-22). Or the time He spoke to the storm, "Peace be still," and it stopped. (Matthew

8:23-27). What about when He walked on the water to the disciples in the boat. (Matthew14:22-33).

He didn't do all those things and more merely on the PREMISE that He was the Son of God. He KNEW Who He was, and He knew it because He remembered.

He didn't have to have faith. He is faith. His faith bears witness with our faith when we believe. Jesus has faith in you that you can fulfill your part of abiding in His vine.

Jesus did miracle after miracle, speaking to His creation, because He knew His creation and His creation knew Him. His creation knew the voice of its Master! How amazing!

Not only did He know His creation, but Jesus knew God as His very own Father before He was placed in Mary's womb by the Holy Spirit.

Remember the time when He told the disciples He saw Satan fall like lightning? (Luke 10:18) How could He see such a thing unless He was there?

I also believe He was the One Who walked with Adam in the cool of the day. (Genesis 3:8)

He, Jesus, is God incarnate. He knew the whole plan of salvation before it all happened. That is why He was able to set His face as a flint to the cross. (Isaiah 50:7). He set His face—meaning He had determined in His heart and mind to finish the goal. He was set. He was fixed. He was determined. And He knew He was the only One Who could do it, because

HE KNEW WHO HE WAS!

JESUS knew He was the perfect plan of salvation, a lamb sent to the slaughter on our behalf.

Jesus knew He was the one and only Son of God. And there was no question in His mind about His authority as the one and only Son of Man on the Earth. Therefore, He had no doubts or questions about His authority. And it showed in everything He did and in everything He said.

Now we, on the other hand, are like sheep—in a pasture—trying to find our way. But Jesus was the Great Shepherd, leading the way. Those sheep who know His voice will follow Him. And those who do not will perish.

As sheep, we are learning about who we are in Him, but He knew Who He was. Jesus was not trying to find His way. Jesus was showing us the way for He is the way.

Jesus explains:

"I tell you the truth, the man who does not enter the sheep pen by the gate, but climbs in by some other way, is a thief and a robber. The man who enters by the gate is the shepherd of his sheep. The watchman opens the gate for him, and the sheep listen to his voice. He calls his own sheep by name and leads them out. When he has brought out all his own, he goes on ahead of them, and his sheep follow him because they know his voice. But they will never follow a stranger; in fact, they will run away from him, because they do not recognize a stranger's voice. Jesus used this figure of speech, but they did not understand what He was telling them."

"Therefore Jesus said again, 'I tell you the truth, I am the gate for the sheep. All who ever came before Me were thieves and robbers, but the sheep did not listen to them. I am the gate (door), whoever enters through Me will be saved. He will come in and go out, and find pasture. The thief comes only to steel and kill and destroy; I have come that they may have life, and have it to the full."

"I am the good Shepherd. The good Shepherd lays down His life for the sheep. The hired hand is not the Shepherd who owns the sheep. So when he sees the wolf coming, he abandons the sheep and runs away. Then the wolf attacks the sheep and scatters them. The man runs away because he is a hired hand and cares nothing for the sheep."

"I am the good Shepherd; I know My sheep, and My sheep now Me – and I lay down My life for the sheep."

"I have other sheep that are not of this sheep pen. I must ring them also. They too will listen to My voice, and there shall be one flock and one Shepherd."

"The reason My Father loves Me is that I lay down My life—only to take it up again. No one takes it from Me, but I lay it down of My own accord. I have Authority to lay it down and Authority to take it up again. This command I received from My Father." John 10:1-18 (NIV).

Jesus is the good Shepherd, and we, like sheep, must follow His voice, His leading, through the friendship of the Holy Spirit.

You see, we grow in our Authority as we learn and receive personal insight about who we are in Him. The more you know Him, the more Authority you have. It is not just head knowledge, but it is heart knowledge from abiding in Him, in His presence, which is the Holy Spirit.

Your personal relationship with the Lord of Glory does not solely depend upon you. The Holy Spirit will draw, speak, inspire, give visions and do whatever He needs to, in order to reveal Himself to you, but you must respond. You must respond to the Holy Spirit. He is there for you, working with you, helping you, and guiding you. He loves you.

> "He (Jesus) said to them, 'But who do you say that I am?' Simon Peter answered and said, 'You are the Christ, the Son of the living God.' Jesus answered and said to him, 'Blessed are you, Simon Bar-Jonah for flesh and blood has not revealed this to you, but My Father who is in Heaven. And I also say to you that you are Peter, and on this rock (this revelation) I will build My church.'" Matthew 16:15.

The rock of revelation is the personal revelation of Who Jesus is in your heart. The more you know Him, the more you know who you are in Him. The more time you spend in His presence, the more personal insight and revelation you will have.

Peter could not have had that revelation without spending time with Jesus. Walking with Jesus totally transformed his life. And when Jesus asked, Peter answered with his very own personal heart revelation. It came from his heart.

Paul said,

"That if you confess with your mouth the Lord Jesus AND BELIEVE IN YOUR HEART that God has raised Him from the dead, you will be saved. For WITH THE HEART ONE BELIEVES unto righteousness (with the heart you come to right standing with God), and with the mouth confession is made unto Salvation (with the confession of your mouth you receive the empowerment of Jesus' sacrifice)." Romans 10:9-10 (Emphasis added).

And Paul said again,

"But I make known to you, brethren, that the gospel which was preached by me is not according to man. For I neither received it from man, nor was I taught it, BUT IT CAME THROUGH THE REVELATION OF JESUS CHRIST." Galatians 1:11-12.

Like I said in the beginning of this chapter, one of the places your Anointing flows is in your secret place of prayer, where you commune and spend time with Him. He loves you, and He wants to spend time with you alone. That is, I believe, the ultimate place He wants to reveal Himself to you—One-on-one.

Get alone with God and pursue Him. Pour out your love to Him. Ask Him to reveal Himself to you, and guess what? He will. He wants to. He is waiting on you. He loves you.

POWER IN YOUR AUTHORITY

Jesus never sinned. "He who knew no sin was made sin for us." 2 Corinthian 5:21.

That gave His Authority great power!

In Matthew, chapter 3, Jesus goes to John to get baptized in water and to receive the Holy Spirit. Then, immediately afterward, in Matthew 4:1-3a:

> "Then Jesus was led up by the (Holy) Spirit into the wilderness to be tempted by the devil. And when He had fasted forty days and forty nights, afterward He was hungry. Now when the tempter came to Him, he said, 'If You are the Son of God.'"

It would seem the devil didn't know who Jesus was. We know, however, that Jesus, being the Son of Man, coming as the Servant of God the Father, would throw the devil completely off. He couldn't be sure who He was, but if he, the devil, could get Jesus to question who He was; if he could get Him to be just a little bit prideful; if He could get Him to just sin one little, itty bitty sin, to fall just one time, then he had Him. Then everything the Father, the Son and the Holy Spirit had worked for would fall apart.

BUT the devil could not touch him! He could not get Him to fall in any way, shape, or form! Because there was no sin found in Jesus! He was absolutely perfect. God's Word incarnate! Thank you Lord, for the Sweet Victory!

Jesus had to be tempted, not just so that God the Father would know what was ultimately in His heart, but Jesus needed to know what was ultimately in His heart, as well.

Why would God the Father need to do such a thing with His very own Son? First of all, because there had been a great rebellion in Heaven. He needed to prove to everyone that there is no greater power than God and His Son.

Secondly, Jesus needed His Authority to have great power, so that He could strip the devil openly of all his Authority and power.

Jesus is our example, and God will allow a man to be tempted for his own growth sake. Being tempted is a test. It is a test so you can grow. God is a good Father. The testing is to show each of us what is within our own heart. This is what gives us personal strength and power in our Authority and Anointing!

Let me put it to you this way. If you were never tested, how would you truly know what was in your heart? How would you know if you could accomplish great things for the Kingdom of God, if you have never gone through anything?

If King David had not had to fight the lion and the bear to save the sheep, he would not have been so confident when it was time for him to slay Goliath.

> "David shouted in reply, 'You come to me with a sword, spear, and javelin, but I come to you in the name of the Lord Almighty—the God of the Armies of Israel, whom you have defied. Today the Lord will conquer you, and I will kill you and cut off your head. And then I will give the dead bodies of your men to the birds and wild animals, and the whole world will know that there is a God in Israel! And everyone will know that the Lord does not need weapons to rescue His people. It is His battle, not ours. The Lord will give you to us.'" 1 Samuel 17:45-57.

This is pretty bold talk for a little redheaded, teenage boy. Why? Because he knew who he was, and he knew what he could do after his tests with the lion and the bear.

When we overcome temptations in our trials, it puts sin in its place—under our feet. And very importantly, it puts the devil under our feet, as well. Each one is just as important as the other, they both, sin and the devil, need to be under our feet.

Let me say it again like this. When we put sin under our feet through obedience, it glorifies God. And when we put the devil under our feet by obeying the Holy Spirit, it really glorifies God! And then guess what? Your Authority increases in power!

When you refuse to sin because you love Jesus, it's pleasing to both you and God the Father. His love is unconditional, but we all can testify that it just feels good when we do the right thing.

It's like the old story of a man popping the buttons on his shirt for the love and pride he takes in his son. His chest swells up with love and pride until his buttons pop off his shirt. It's an overwhelming, over the top feeling you have for your children in your heart and in your chest, when they do something you are really proud of them for doing. It's very real. I've experienced it for my children.

So when we make Godly decisions, God is glorified like that through your obedience, and the devil is humiliated under your feet! He is humiliated! I love it! Let's humiliate the devil and follow the Holy Spirit!

Is this scriptural? Yes!

"Therefore let him who thinks he stands, take heed lest he fall. (In other words—watch out if you don't think you can fall into sin, because God is going to test you to see what is in your heart. He wants you to grow in the POWER of "your" anointing!!!) No temptation has overtaken you except such as is common to man (you are not the only one who has ever been tempted this way); BUT (don't lose heart) GOD IS FATIHFUL!!! who will not allow you to be tempted beyond what you are able, but with the temptation (God) will also make the way of escape (for you!) so that you may be able to bear it. (Because He loves you!) 1 Corinthians 10:12-13 (AMP, Emphasis added).

But are you going to take the way of escape? When that trial comes, the test, are you going to stand your ground for righteousness? What is really in your heart? What are you really going to do?

Once you have been tempted and you have taken the way of escape, you, YOUR INNER MAN, then becomes STRONG in the Lord and in the POWER of His might. (Ephesians 6:10). You become strong in the Authority Jesus has given you, which backs up the POWER of His Anointing, His might in you!

The key words here are Authority and power. GOD WANTS YOUR AUTHORITY TO HAVE GREAT POWER! God wants your Anointing, the manifested presence of the Holy Spirit, to have great power in your walk with Him and on your gifts! He wants YOU to be strong in who you are in Jesus. He wants YOU to be ROCK SOLID CONCRETE in who you are in Jesus!

You don't have to wonder, after you have been tested and passed the test, then you KNOW who you are.

Godly character is rare to find, but great in power.

If you don't pass the test, then you will probably have to go back and retake it until you do. And then, if you still don't pass, you could ultimately forfeit what God has for you.

God is longsuffering and patient with you. He wants you to know who you are, because if you know who you are then your Authority has great power.

I've often told the Lord in my walk with Him: "God, if I only knew what was going on, I would be able to bear it." And so here it is—a little secret about the Father. He loves you as His own, because you ARE His own! So as your Heavenly Father, he allows you to be put into situations that will cause you to grow. No test, no growth. No test, no increase in power. No test, no increase in your Anointing, and no power in your Authority.

Since you belong to Him, He only wants the best for you. That means, in order to get your spirit-man to grow and excel and to be the best you could possibly be, there needs to be some pressure in your life.

As a musician, it is the pressure of performing that makes you a great musician. It's a lifetime of work, a lifetime of preparing and becoming your best.

As an athlete it is the pressure of performing that makes you a great athlete. It's a lifetime of work, a lifetime of preparing and becoming your best.

As a Christian, it is the pressures or the trials of your life that can make you a strong and great follower of Jesus. It's a lifetime of walking with the Holy Spirit, and a lifetime of yielding to the Holy Spirit that aids you in becoming your best in Him.

However, the choice is yours. You can yield to the Holy Spirit, or you can kick and complain the whole way, wish things were different, and never get where you need to be in Him or in life.

Your tests put you in a position to especially deal with the day-to-day things that bug you on a different level.

Because of the pressures of what you are going through, you can be mean and quick to hurt others, or you can humble yourself and be kind, especially when you don't want to. Humble yourself, and let the fruit of the Holy Spirit work in you.

The fruit of the Spirit and your soul are trying to become one. Your soul is conforming to the fruit of the Spirit by yielding to Him, the Holy Spirit. This grace is sufficient to help you, but to help you in your obedience to His drawing and His leading.

It is His grace that empowers you to do the task at hand. His grace empowers you to walk in obedience to His Word. And His grace empowers you to receive His fruit of the Spirit which is love, joy, peace, patience, kindness, goodness, faithfulness, gentleness and self-control. (Galatians 5:22).

It is the trials of this life that prove to us what we are really made of. It proves to us who we really are.

What kind of Godly character do you have? Without the fellowship and help of the Holy Spirit we'd never get very far. Why? It's simply because we cannot do it on our own.

We need the Holy Spirit!

"Endure hardship as discipline; God is treating you as sons." Hebrews 12:7 (NIV).

"As many as I love, I rebuke and chasten. Therefore be zealous and repent. Behold, I stand at the door and knock. If anyone hears My voice and opens the door, I will come in to him and dine with him, and he with Me." Revelation 3:19-20.

Jesus is talking to believers here. He said to be zealous and repent. That means to get right with God and be thankful! Show Him how thankful you are by using your gifts and yielding to the work of the Holy Spirit. The more you do it, the easier it becomes. It is in your best interest to yield your tongue and your actions to the Holy Spirit, and then you will bear the fruit of the Spirit.

> "Therefore by Him (Jesus) let us continually offer the sacrifice of praise to God, that is the fruit of our lips, giving thanks to His name, and do not forget to do good and to share, for with such sacrifices God is well pleased." Hebrews 13:15.

The Holy Spirit is standing at the door, knocking. He wants to come in and dine with you. He wants to have fellowship with you.

He is called the helper for a reason. He is not only your helper, but your counselor and best friend. He is your Anointing! His presence living in you, manifesting in your secret place of prayer, and in your gifts, is for you!

If you want to be an overcomer and inherit the purpose, the plans, the calling, the destiny, and the things God has in His heart for you, then you must be in daily fellowship with the Holy Spirit and His Anointing. He will put things in order in your life for you, but you must follow and be attentive to His leading.

> "My thoughts toward you are for good and not evil. To give you a hope and a future." Jeremiah 29:11.

> "Jesus said, 'You can enter God's Kingdom only through the narrow gate. The highway to hell is broad, and its gate is wide for the many who choose the EASY way. BUT THE GATEWAY TO LIFE IS SMALL, AND THE ROAD IS NARROW, AND ONLY A FEW EVER FIND IT." Matthew 7:13-14 (NLT).

When I was growing up, there was an old saying I would sometimes hear, "You are so narrow-minded." But the fact is, it's because the road to life is narrow, and I want to be one of the few who find it!

> "So let us press, and let us run the race with diligence!" Acts 20:24; 1 Corinthians 9:24-27; Hebrews 12:1-2; 2 Timothy 3:6-8.

So, your Authority grows in power as you separate yourself from sin. The less you sin, the more power you have in your Authority.

YOUR ANOINTING IS VITAL

> "Now GOD worked unusual miracles by the hands of Paul, so that even handkerchiefs or aprons were brought from his body to the sick, and the diseases left them and the evil spirits went out of them."

> "Then some of the itinerant Jewish exorcists took it upon themselves to call the name of the Lord Jesus over those who had evil spirits, saying 'We exorcise you by the Jesus whom Paul preaches.' Also, there were the seven sons of Sceva, a Jewish chief priest, who did so; And the evil spirit answered and said, 'Jesus I know, and Paul I know; but who are you?' Then, the man in whom the evil spirit was, leaped on them, overpowered them, and prevailed against them, so much so that they fled out of that house naked and wounded."

"This became known both to all Jews and Greeks dwelling in Ephesus; and fear fell on them all, and the name of the Lord Jesus was magnified. And many who had believed came confessing and telling their deeds. Also, many of those who had practiced magic brought their books together and burned them in the sight of all. And they counted up the value of them, and it totaled fifty thousand pieces of silver. So the word of the Lord grew mightily and prevailed." Acts 19:11-20.

Why did this happen? Well, of course, God took something the devil meant for evil and turned it for good, and His Kingdom was glorified then, just as it is to this day!

But the demon said, "Jesus I know, and Paul I know, but who are you?" Why did the demon ask who they were? Because he didn't recognize them. Both Jesus and Paul had the baptism of the Holy Spirit. (1 Corinthians 14:18). They both had the Seal of Approval. They both had the Authority through the Anointing of the Holy Spirit to cast out demons. And the demon did not see that Seal of Authority, the Holy Spirit's Anointing, in or on the men who were trying to exorcise them.

These men had good intentions. They wanted to help someone get free from demons. I'm sure they thought that as the sons of a Jewish chief priest, they had the Authority.

But unless you have God's Seal of Approval, THE HOLY SPIRIT'S ANOINTING, you cannot successfully use the "Authority" that comes in the Name of Jesus! It doesn't matter who you are or what you do for a living.

That Authority is a gift! Jesus gives us His Seal of Approval, His Authority, the baptism of the Holy Spirit's Anointing, when we have had the faith to become born again, but it's not until then. You must be born again to receive the baptism of the Holy Spirit.

Jesus did not do any miracles until after He had been baptized in the Holy Spirit Anointing. If anyone could have done miracles without the Holy Spirit Anointing, it would have been Him! But He did not!

Think about it. The only way miracles can be worked here on the Earth is through the Power of the Anointing of the Holy Spirit, God Almighty's manifested presence on the Earth. Only God Almighty has true power. Only God Almighty's presence through the Holy Spirit is true power on the Earth.

Jesus was raised from the dead by God the Father through the Holy Spirit's power. Jesus did not raise Himself from the dead. God's power on the Earth is through the Holy Spirit's Anointing and that is Who raised Jesus from the dead. He did not do it on His own. It does not make Jesus any less the Son of God, nor does it take away from the fact that He, all by Himself, as the Son of Man, lived a life on this Earth without any kind of sin.

We do not see the spirit realm with our natural eyes. We walk by faith. Having faith in Jesus is huge! If you can believe in Jesus and receive your gift, the Seal of Authority which is the Anointing of the Holy Spirit, then nothing can stop you! And since we walk by faith and not by sight, that gives God great glory.

The devil cannot fight against God's glory. The devil cannot fight against God's Authority, which is the power you have in the Holy Spirit's Anointing.

Have faith in Jesus! God knows what He is doing. Receive the Holy Spirit, and receive God's Anointing, which is His manifested power for you. You need the Holy Spirit.

Those who live in the spirit realm, (the angels, and demons, and all the other living creatures,) they see. They can tell if you have been born-again. They can tell if you have the Seal of Authority, the Holy Spirit! They can tell if you are living in your God-given Authority, your Anointing. It shows.

Yes! Your Anointing is vital!

Now let's recap the vision:

I was riding on a white horse, along side of the Lord Jesus, Who was also riding on a white horse. There were thousands of others as far as the eye could see, who were also riding beside us and behind us on white horses. We were all dressed in "white uniform-like for battle" clothes, none were exactly alike, absolutely beautiful and immaculate, and so were the horses. We were coming down out of the sky on our way to what seemed to be a great battle, and the Lord was leading the way.

I can't say the Holy Spirit spoke to me. It was an overall knowing all at once when He dropped the interpretation of the dream in me.

"My horse, the one I was riding on, represented my place of Authority in Him. My place of Authority is my Anointing. My Anointing is what I am gifted in. And my gift is the call on my life."

My horse is a gift. It is my place of Authority in Jesus. I have a place of Authority in Jesus. It's real. That horse, like the dove that appeared on Jesus when He was baptized, is God the Father's Seal of Approval for me.

Imagine God saying this to you, "Here, have this horse. It's for you. It is My Authority; My gift to you. Everywhere you go on your horse you will have My Authority. You can speak and do what you need to with me backing you up with My Authority. It is My presence with you. When people see you riding up on your horse, they see My Authority is with you."

Your horse, your place of Authority is the gift of the Holy Spirit. He is your Seal of Approval. Jesus approves you because you received His sacrifice He made for you, and now your sins are forgiven, and you are in right-standing with God the Father. God the Father approves of you, because you believe in His Son and have received Him as your Savior.

I am going to tell you something you must receive. Without the Holy Spirit Anointing, you have no Authority!

Jesus said to "receive the Holy Spirit" and then you can go in His Authority.

You can use His Name all day long, but until you have the Authority to use it, it will accomplish nothing.

So receive the baptism of the Holy Spirit. Let Him lead you and guide you into all truth. Let your relationship with Him grow. Seek Him. Desire Him more than life itself, for He is life. And He will show Himself strong on your behalf.

> "Seek first the Kingdom of God and His righteousness! And all these things will be added unto you!" Matthew 6:33.

> "But without faith it is impossible to please Him, for He who comes to God must believe that He is, and that He is a rewarder to those who diligently seek Him" Hebrews 11:6.

Chapter 3

WHAT IS YOUR ANOINTING

What is "your" Anointing? Your personal Anointing is the manifested presence of the Holy Spirit on your gifts, talents, and abilities.

In the last chapter, I talked to you about the Authority you have in your Anointing. But now I want to talk to you specifically about the personal flow you have in the Holy Spirit. How it's powerful and unique to you.

Don't forget! You have Authority in your Anointing. When the Holy Spirit's anointing manifests through your gifts, you are able to flow in "your" special place of Authority. It is a place of Authority that God has supernaturally given to you personally. It is special to you. There is no one else who can move in that Anointing like you can. It is an Authority "You" have! No one else can take it away from you or duplicate it, because it is a part of who you are. It's in your DNA.

There is no one else living where you live, doing what you do, and influencing the people you influence. Your

Anointing is unique to you to where you live, to what you do, and to the people who are in your life.

Ponder and think about it! Selah!

I'm talking specifically about "you" here. I am talking about "your" Anointing, which is the manifested presence of the Holy Spirit flowing freely in your life.

I love how it all flows together. How your Authority, your Anointing, your gifts and your call all flow together as one. God is smart. This is all very mindful and strategic in His heart. He is in the central control of everything. He is working it all together for your good and for the good of the Body of Christ. He knows what He is doing!

Yes! Everyone is special to God! Everyone has gifts and talents that God has especially ordained for them.

God started with Adam and Eve. He placed in them unique abilities, and gifts that were theirs for the time they lived here on the Earth, and now through all of eternity. He has also placed in all of us unique abilities and gifts for the times we live in here, and for all eternity.

He is so awesome, so creative, and so beyond us! His ability to create everything uniquely different and special is just amazing! All the way down to even snowflakes! I love it! Let's give honor to Whom honor is due. He is the Creator!

God gave you your gifts and talents before you were born. As a matter of fact, He knew you before you were born.

You were in His heart before He even started His creation!
You, YOU, were a light of inspiration in His heart!

"All things were made through Him, and without
Him nothing was made that was made." (That's
you!) "In Him was life, and the life was the light
of men." (And that's you, too!) John 1:3-4.

1) He has illuminated you with His life!
2) He has made all of "Who He is" available to you.
3) I'm going to say it again, YOU are His inspiration!
   Alleluia!

According to Vine's Expository Dictionary of New
Testament Words, "the light and life of God" from
John 1:3-4:
   The Glory of His Dwelling Place!
   His Nature or Who He is!
   The impartiality of Who He is!
   His favor!
   His Rulership!
   The illuminator of His people!

You see, His life and His light are Who He is!
He was watching over your seed of faith before you
were born. He was inspired when you were born. He was

inspired again when you were born again, and now He is watching over you, to do good things for you.

"Being confident of this very thing, that He who has begun a good work in you will complete it until the day of Jesus Christ." Philippians 1:6.

Some gifts and talents are more obvious than others, but they are all of great value to God.

YOU are of great value to God. Your gifts and your talents are of great value to God, and He has strategically given them to you for you to enjoy and grow in.

If you want to be a blessing to God, then grow in your gifts and talents. He loves it when you do, because He loves you! (John 3:16)

As I am sure you already know the Bible talks about our spiritual gifts God has given us.

"Having then gifts differing according to the grace that is given to us, let us use them; if prophecy, let us prophesy in proportion to our faith; or ministry, let us use it in our ministering; he who teaches, in teaching; he who exhorts, in exhortation; he who gives, with liberality; he who leads, with diligence; he who shows mercy, with cheerfulness." Romans 12:6.

There have been all kinds of studies and books and tests about the spiritual gifts mentioned in the Bible. And it is for that reason I am not going to cover it all. It's already been done. However, here is a list of them:

1. Evangelism
2. Prophecy
3. Teaching
4. Exhortation
5. Pastor/Shepherd
6. Showing Mercy
7. Serving
8. Giving
9. Administration/Leadership

I do highly recommend that you take the test to find out what your gifts are. Go online to: Church Growth Institute. Take the test and find out all kinds of neat stuff about yourself. It will help you find out why you are the way you are, why you do the things you do, and what makes you tick! It is a very useful tool to have.

I was always told I was very prophetic, so I assumed my spiritual gift was a prophet. Boy, was I ever wrong. After I recently took the test, I found out my main two gifts were pastor and administration, and the very last thing on my list was prophet! Go figure. I think it's funny.

I believe one of the greatest joys the Holy Spirit has is helping you and inspiring you in your gifts and talents. The Holy Spirit is our mentor. He is our guide.

Let's look at 1 John 2:20, 27, 17b in the AMP.
"But you have been anointed by (you hold a sacred appointment from, you have been given an unction from) the Holy One (the Holy Spirit), and you all know (the Truth) (Jesus)."

What is that unction? It is the Anointing. What is that sacred appointment? It is the Anointing.

So since you know the truth, and Jesus is the truth, He has set you free! He has given your spirit, soul, and body a freedom that is not available to the world. And in that freedom, He gives His Seal of Approval, the Holy Spirit. In the Holy Spirit is your Holy Oil, your Holy Anointing Oil, your unction, your sacred appointment.

That leading, that unction, that tangible, warm Holy Oil presence of the Holy Spirit is what produces the results you are looking for and waiting for.

Let's look at verse 27,
"But for you, the Anointing (the sacred appointment, the unction) which you received from Him (from Who? From the Holy Spirit) abides (permanently) IN YOU; (so) then you

have no need that anyone should instruct you. But just as His Anointing teaches you concerning every-thing and is true and is no falsehood (or a lie), so you must abide in (live in, and never depart from) Him (being rooted in Him, (and) knit to Him), just as (His Anointing) has taught you (to do)."

Now let's look at the last part of verse 17, "But he who does the will of God and carries out His purposes in his life abides (remains) forever."

So what is the will of God for you? His will for you is to abide and walk with Him. To do that you must live in the fellowship of His Holy Spirit and His Anointing; everything else will flow out of that. Matthew 6:33.

What is His purpose for your life? He wants you to grow and use the wonderful gifts and talents He has given you under the influence of the Anointing and the fellowship of the Holy Spirit. In that, you will further the gospel of His Kingdom.

Let's go to John 14:16-18a, where Jesus is talking to His disciples:

"And I will pray to the Father, and He will give you another Helper, that He may abide with you forever—the Spirit of truth (which is the Holy Spirit), whom the world cannot receive, because it neither sees Him nor knows Him; but you know Him, for He dwells with you and will be in you. I will not leave you orphans."

Now in John 15:4, Jesus is still talking to His disciples and He says,

"Abide in Me, and I in you. As the branch cannot bear fruit of itself, unless it abides in the vine, neither can you, unless you abide in Me."

Now remember, your Authority is your Anointing, your Anointing is what you are gifted in and your gifts and your talents are what establish the calling on your life.

Sometimes, it's hard to see what He is doing with your life, until you are close to the end of your journey, and then you can look back at what He has done. But the Holy Spirit will lead you, guide you, teach you and be your best friend through this life. And your gifts are a great part of that.

Chapter 4

YOUR SPIRITUAL GIFTS

Let's look at what makes you—you. God has creatively made us into three distinctive parts: spirit, soul and body.

Your spirit is your innermost being, not to be confused with your soul. When you become born again, which means your spirit-man has become alive to God, your spirit only knows the truth. It does not know falsehood of any kind. It cannot know evil, because it has become one with God, Who is perfect and Holy.

Your spirit has its own function. It communes with God. That is why spending time alone with God through the Holy Spirit's presence in you is so important. You need to commune with God. Your spirit-man needs that in order to grow. This is where you really grow in God. It is also why it is so important to use your spiritual gifts in the secret place of prayer. This is the best place for them to grow before you use them somewhere else.

Once your spirit-man becomes born again, Jesus rewards you openly with His gift of Authority, because you have openly confessed Him as your Savior. Your gift of

Authority is the Holy Spirit. The Holy Spirit is the Anointing. It is the Holy Spirit Who gives you personal revelation and insight of Who Jesus is, which in turn helps you know who you are in Him. It is the Holy Spirit Who has the Spiritual gifts you need to grow.

Jesus said, "When the Spirit of Truth comes, He will guide you into all truth. For He will not speak on His own Authority (He will not be presenting His own ideas), but whatever He hears He will speak; and He will tell you of things to come (the future)." John 16:13 NKJ and NLT.

Paul explains about your Spiritual gifts in 1 Corinthians 12:1, 4-11:

> "Now concerning Spiritual gifts, brethren, I do not want you to be ignorant: There are diversities of gifts, but the same Spirit. There are differences of ministries, but the same Lord. And there are diversities of activities, but it is the same God who works all in all. But the manifestation of the Spirit is given to each one for the profit of all: for to one is given the word of wisdom through the Spirit, to another the word of knowledge through the same Spirit, to another faith by the same Spirit, to another gifts of healings by the same Spirit, to another the working of miracles, to another prophecy, to another discerning of spirits, to another different kinds of tongues, to another

the interpretation of tongues, But one and the same Spirit works all these things, distributing to each one individually as He wills."

Yes, the gifts of the Holy Spirit are for you. They are the presence of His Anointing flowing through you. He can inspire you with His wisdom, when you need to know what to do. Or He can inspire you with His knowledge when you need to know how to do something. And in your secret place of prayer or when you are with others, He can inspire you with faith to believe Him for whatever the situation is you are in.

His Anointing and His gifts give you what you need for whatever the circumstances are in your life. He is there to help you.

Now, His gifts will flow in your personal gifts, talents, and abilities—His wisdom, His knowledge, His inspiration of faith, His working of miracles, His insight to prophecy, His ability to discern, His speaking threw you in a language you don't know, and then His ability to tell you what was said! Wow! He is so awesome! It is all the Holy Spirit working these wonderful inspirations in you and through you, for you and for others.

And now your soul: your soul, as most of us have heard, is your mind, will, and emotions. It is your personality. This is where your personal gifts and talents, your conscience and imagination flow from.

The Holy Spirit's inspirational gifts, I was talking about in your spirit, flow into your soul's gifts and talents.

Your soul is what determines how much Anointing, revelation, and fruit you have in your life. It determines how much of the Holy Spirit's inspirations flow in your life. And it happens by the communion or abiding you have with the Holy Spirit.

Your soul, you, must learn how to allow the Holy Spirit to flow in you and through you. In many cases, it's called yielding to the Holy Spirit.

Do you want to know Him more? (your thoughts) Has your heart made the decision to learn and retain more knowledge about Him? (your will) Are you open to feeling His presence and being led by Him? (emotions) And have you predetermined how you will respond to His presence? (with your mind, your will, and your emotions) Will you listen and follow Him?

Once you have received the baptism of the Holy Spirit, your Authority takes on a whole new dynamic, a whole new dimension. Then the Holy Spirit's constant presence is with you, and your soul has the constant influence of the Holy Spirit and His Anointing. How wonderful! We need that.

Yes! This is when your gifts take on a whole new dynamic! A whole new dynamo! A whole new power! It's very exciting to think that God will empower who you are in your personal gifts and talents with His Anointing!

Chapter 5

USING YOUR GIFTS—TALENTS

In the Bible Jesus told a story about three men who were given talents or gifts from their master.

"For the Kingdom of Heaven is like a man traveling to a far country, who called his own servants and delivered his goods to them. And to one he gave five talents, to another two, and to another one, to each according to his own ability; and immediately he went on a journey. Then he who had received the five talents went and traded with them, and made another five talents. And likewise he who had received two gained two more also. But he who had received one went and dug in the ground, and hid his lord's money. After a long time the lord of those servants came and settled accounts with them. So he who had received five talents came and brought five other talents, saying, 'Lord, you delivered to me five talents; look I have gained five more talents besides them.' His lord said to him, 'Well done, good and faithful servant; you were faithful over a few things, I will make you ruler over many things. Enter into the joy of your lord.' He also who had received two talents came and said, 'Lord, you delivered to me two talents; look, I have gained two more talents besides them.' His lord said to him, 'Well done, good and faithful servant; you have been faithful over a few things. Enter into the joy of your Lord.' Then he who had received the one talent came and said, 'Lord, I knew you to be a hard man, reaping where you have not sown, and gathering where you have no scattered seed. And I was afraid, and went and hid your talent in the ground. Look, there you have what is yours.' BUT his lord answered and said to him, 'You wicked and lazy servant. You knew that I reap where I have not sown, and gather where I have not scattered seed. So you ought to have deposited my money with the bankers, and at my coming I would have received back my own with interest. Therefore take the talent from him and give it to him who has ten talents. For to everyone who has, more will be given, and he will have abundance; but from him who does not have even what he has will be taken away.

And cast the unprofitable servant into the outer darkness. There will be weeping and gnashing of teeth.'" Matthew 25:14-30.

This is the challenge we have even today. The King, Jesus, has given us gifts and talents and abilities to fulfill the calling on our lives. What are we going to do with what He has given us?

Think about it. What are you going to do with what He has given you? From this Scripture we can surmise that there are three groups of people in the world. All I know is that I don't want to be in the last group! So let's start with the last group, the third servant. We need to learn this valuable lesson, so it doesn't happen to us.

"The Kingdom of God—The KINGDOM of God—It is not meat and drink. But it is righteousness, and peace, and joy in the Holy Ghost!" Romans 14:17.

The King of the Kingdom, or as in this story the Lord of the Kingdom, reaped where he did not sow because he was the King. It makes sense. The King reaps where he does not sow, and He gathers where he does not scatter seed. Why? Because He is the King of the Kingdom! It all belongs to Him!

The Scripture says, "For the Kingdom of Heaven is like a man traveling to a far country, who called his own servants and delivered his goods to them … To each to his own ability."

Even though the third servant was a servant to the King, he did not know the King or Who He was. He only perceived the King to be a hard man—reaping where He did not sow and gathering where He did not scatter seed.

The Kingdom of God is righteousness, which is being in right-standing with the King. It is peace, which is a knowing that you are in a right-standing position with the King. And it is the joy of being in fellowship with the King through His Holy Spirit.

THIS KINGDOM OF GOD IS ABOUT KNOWING THE KING! That is the whole thrust of God's Kingdom—KNOWING HIM!

The big lie has been that He is not tangible. But THAT IS the big lie! He is very tangible. When you ask Him to forgive you of your sins, that reality is very real! When He comes and resides within you, that is very real and tangible. At that moment, when you become born again, His love for you sets your heart and soul free! Yes! It is very real, and it is very tangible. No one can do that for you, but God! His presence is very real and His Anointing is for you!

The Scripture says:

"The beginning of wisdom is the fear or the respect of the Lord." Proverbs 9:10.

"The fear of the Lord is the instruction of wisdom." Proverbs 15:33.

As Christians, the fear we have for Him is that of GREAT respect. We do and don't do things out of the respect we have for Him because of Who He is. We stop sinning or even have the desire to sin, once we become born again, because we respect Him, and we love Him. That love and respect comes from what He has done for us. What He has done for us is beyond our understanding! That love and respect comes from Who He is. And Who He is, is beyond our comprehension! His love for us is absolutely amazing!

He is the Great Creator of all the solar systems in outer space, of the stars, the planets, the Earth, and all that they are. He is the King of Glory, Who came to the Earth to live a sinless life for us and then to die a cruel death on the Cross for our sins! He was raised from the dead and walked among his disciples and many people for 40 days, so there would be no question that He was raised from the dead. And now, He sits at the right hand of the Father, constantly watching us and talking to the Father on our behalf. Wow! I must say this! He is the Great God of love, mercy and goodness!

This third servant, even though he was a servant to the King, he could not respond in a positive way to the King.

As previously mentioned, the Kingdom of God is righteousness, being in right-standing with the King. This servant was obviously not in right-standing with the King, so the King reached out to him and gave him an opportunity to get in a right-standing place with Him, to show Him that he had respect for Him.

Each servant was given a talent according to his own ability. This servant had the ability to do something, but refused to do it. He did nothing to change the circumstances he was in or the relationship he had with the King! The King gave him a GREAT opportunity to do something, but he chose to do nothing. He buried his opportunity in the ground! What a waist. He refused to show the King any kind of respect at all.

Even the King said he could have put it in the bank and had given Him the interest on it. How much effort was that? The interest was what? It was the tithe. But he dug a hole in the ground, and he hid it! It doesn't make any sense! What a great opportunity he had, but he was too lazy to do anything about it!

> "But this I say, 'He who sows sparingly will also reap sparingly, and he who sows bountifully will also, reap bountifully.'" 2 Corinthians 9:6.

Let me say it like this: If you sow nothing, you can expect nothing in return.

When you are a Kingdom person you want to please the King. Even the principal of tithing falls into this third servant's hands. Tithing was nothing new. It has been practiced since before Abraham. He knew about tithing. Had he put what the King gave him in the bank, he would have had at the least a tithe to give Him.

Everyone has a choice. Anyone who wants to know the King has the opportunity. It's there. Anyone who wants to please the King, or to show Him respect, the opportunity is still there. Especially like this servant. I believe this is a lesson not just for those who claim to be His, but for the lost, as well.

In the New Testament there is a story about a man who gave to the poor out of his mercy for the poor and out of his respect for God. Alleluia! God in return told him his gifts and his alms had come up before Him as a memorial. Yes, I'm talking about Cornelius. God knows and takes into account your efforts of showing mercy to the poor and Him respect!

This story is in Acts, chapter 10. Cornelius and his family were the first among the gentiles to receive the baptism of the Holy Spirit, the precious fellowship and Anointing of the Holy Spirit! His name and testimony was written about in the Bible for millions to read and to see throughout all eternity. God will bless those who show Him respect and who are merciful to the poor.

God wanted to have fellowship with Cornelius and his family, because of his heart toward the poor and his respect for God. He revealed Himself to them and blessed them many times over in return.

What was the King's response to this third servant? The King said the servant was wicked and lazy, and then gave his talent to the man who had already doubled what was given to him and was given more than the others.

And then he said,

"For to everyone who has, more will be given, and he will have abundance. But from him who does not have even what he has will be taken away. (So now) cast the UNPROFITABLE servant into the outer darkness. (Where) there will be weeping and gnashing of teeth."

Jesus, the King of the Kingdom, is the righteous judge.

"So then, since Christ suffered physical pain, you must arm yourselves with the same attitude he had, and be ready to suffer, too. For if you are willing to suffer for Christ, you have decided to stop sinning. And you won't spend the rest of your life chasing after evil desires, but you will be anxious to do the will of God. You have had enough in the past of the evil things that godless people enjoy—their immorality and lust, their feasting and drunkenness and wild parties, and their terrible worship of idols.

"Of course, your former friends are very surprised when you no longer join them in the wicked things they do, and they say evil things about you. But just remember that they will have to face God, Who will judge everyone, both the living and the dead.

"Therefore, be earnest and disciplined in your prayers. Most important of all, continue to show deep love for each other, for love covers a multitude of sins …

"God has given gifts to each of you from His great variety of spiritual gifts. Manage them well so that God's generosity can flow through you.

"Are you called to be a speaker? Then speak as though God Himself were speaking through you. Are you called to help others? Do it with all the strength and energy that God supplies. Then God will be glorified in everything through Jesus Christ. All glory and power belong to Him forever and ever. Amen."
1 Peter 4:1-5, 7b-8, 10—11 NLT.

"For we know Him Who said, 'Vengeance is Mine, I will repay' says the Lord. And again, 'The Lord will judge His people.' It is a fearful thing to fall into the hands of the living God." Hebrews 10:30-31.

"Truly, these times of ignorance God overlooked, but now commands all men everywhere to repent, because He has appointed a day on which He will judge the world in righteousness by raising Him from the dead." Acts 17:30-31.

So, apparently, if you choose not to do anything about what God has given you, if you choose to turn your back and not receive the free gift of salvation, if you choose not to show any kind of respect to the King of the Kingdom, the end result is torment, and eternity in a place that was not created for you.

You must know that He is worthy of your respect. And it is an Honor to be in fellowship with the King. So show Him respect, and do something with what He has given you.

There is a day of judgment coming even for His servants. We must be aware that we are not exempt from being judged for what we have done. We are not without responsibility. Yes, it is the working of the Holy Spirit in our lives, but it is our responsibility to respond to Him to follow through with the dreams he has put in our hearts. We must walk with Him, not against Him. We need to stop kicking and screaming the whole way. Walk, abide, and draw on Him. Draw on His Anointing, His encouragement, His strength. Remember, the last thing He told you to do. And, do it!

There are people of the world, whether they do well financially or not, it has no bearing, but there are people of the world who refuse to believe in God. They refuse to believe He is good. There are those who refuse to believe that He even exists! God, Himself says,

> "Only a fool would say in his heart, there is no God." Psalms 14:1; 53:1; Proverbs 28:26.

Those people will lead you off into a ditch every time. Don't even entertain their philosophy of thinking. Proverbs 18:2; 26:4. Evil will always try to corrupt good.

> "Do not be deceived, 'Evil company corrupts good habits,' Awake to righteousness, and do not sin; for some do not have the knowledge of God. I speak this to your shame."
> 1 Corinthians 15:33-34.

As my husband would say, "Don't get in the ditch with them." Follow the Holy Spirit; He will never lead you the wrong way.

I've often heard people say, "God knows my heart."
Yes, He knows your heart, and unfortunately, so does
everyone else. It's obvious. You either live for Him or you
don't. You either have Godly character and good fruit in your
life, or you have worldly character and bad fruit in your life.
It's the latter that brings death to you and to others around
you, especially the people you love. You can unintentionally
lead the people you love into a ditch. Don't lie to yourself and
pretend everything is okay when it's not. There is good fruit
and there is bad fruit. The Lord Jesus talked about it.

> "For a good tree does not bear bad fruit, nor does
> a bad tree bear good fruit. For every tree is known
> by its own fruit. For men do not gather figs from
> thorns, nor do they gather grapes from a bramble
> bush. A good man out of the good treasure of
> his heart brings forth good, and an evil man out
> of the evil treasure of his heart brings forth evil.
> For out of the abundance of the heart his mouth
> speaks." Luke 6:43-45.

Now when it comes to the gifts and talents the Lord
has given us, the people in the third group don't do anything
with what they have.

These are the people who always seem to have their
hands out. They wait for someone else to do the work for them.

They are unable to make decisions for themselves. They seem to have no inspiration or ambition in their lives. They live in fear of what could go wrong. They try to get by with doing as little as possible. That kind of lifestyle is not pleasing to God, and frankly, it is not pleasing to anyone. I refuse to feel sorry for people who don't do anything out of sheer laziness.

Remember, the Lord said he gave them talents according to their own ability. So the man who was given one talent had the ability to do something with it, but refused to. It's as if he had an attitude toward the Lord for giving him the opportunity. He judged the Lord and said He was a hard man. There was an old saying I heard while growing up, "Sometimes, you are your own worst enemy." His lack of enthusiasm and thankfulness for the opportunity did not hold water on the day he had to give an account.

"Shall the pot tell the potter he is doing it wrong?"
Isaiah 29:16; 64:8.

God has given everyone gifts and talents. There is no excuse for laziness. And there will be no excuses when we see Him face-to-face. He made a way for us all to know Him. He has given us opportunities to grow in our gifts and talents. It's up to us to do something with them. It's up to us to pursue what He has given us.

In the beginning, when Adam fell, the Lord told him, "Now you will have to work for everything." It's like the old saying, "Anything worth having is worth working for."

So, let us work, let us pursue, and let us go for God! He is worth it, and He deserves it.

Chapter 6

BEARING MUCH FRUIT

As we continue in Matthew 25:14-30, the Word reveals that the next two servants were very much alike. The Lord of the Kingdom gave them what He knew they could work with, according to their own ability. In return, their gifts, and their talents were used to give the King glory. They took the opportunity the King had given them and pursued it. They both did the best they could with what was given to them and they both doubled it.

They both showed Him respect, and love, and gratitude for the opportunity by doubling what He had given them.

Now don't forget, we are talking about our anointing. Your personal anointing is the gifts, talents, and abilities the King of the Kingdom, Jesus, has given you.

It takes work to bear much fruit. It takes work to bring increase. You must be diligent and steadfast to pursue the Kingdom of God with your gifts and talents.

The first servant was given five talents, and he doubled it to ten. That's the guy we all want to be like. But it really doesn't matter if you are the first guy or not. As long as you are faithful with what the King has given you, you will receive the same wonderful words. "Well done, good and faithful servant! Enter into the Joy of the Kingdom!"

He has only given you what you are capable of working with. But then there seems to be a group of people who go over the top with what was given to them. Who are those guys?

I remember an old movie called *Butch Cassidy and the Sundance Kid*. It was a western, so they were outlaws, of course. They successfully robbed a train, but when they tried to rob their second train, the company who owned it was prepared for them. A posse came barreling out of the back of the train to pursue them. For weeks the posse chased them, and then gave up, except for two guys. These guys were able to track them, no matter where they went. The outlaws wondered and repeatedly asked, "Who are those guys?"

They finally came to the conclusion it was the renowned Indian tracker, Lord Baltimore and the relentless lawman, Joe LeFors. These men had a reputation of being relentless. They were determined to come back with their prize, and nothing was going to stop them. After being chased from Wyoming to Bolivia, the outlaws finally came to their death in a big fight.

Now, we are talking again about bearing much fruit!

Who are those guys? They are the relentless ones. They are determined. There is a prize, and they want it. They have become the best at what they do and will not stop until they have reached their goal. They will not be denied.

It takes time, energy and work to accomplish what the King has given you to do.

But, let me pose a thought for you. There seems to be a group of outstanding "leaders" in all walks of life who carry a load we do not know about. It's a side of them that only their closest loved ones know about. No, really. Maybe there is a heart rending price to pay to be like one of those guys.

For example: Paul had a thorn in his side, but he also had great revelation and the talent to communicate it. He pursued the Kingdom of God and His righteousness first. He did his best to show the King respect, love, and gratitude. As a result, he bore much fruit!

There is a lot of depth to Paul. He wasn't just the "average Joe."

We don't really know what his thorn was. We could guess. Maybe it was the sorrow of helping to have believers of Christ Jesus persecuted and murdered before he had his own personal experience with Jesus. That is huge! Or maybe it was the loss of his family for the gospel's sake. That is huge, too! Or maybe it was his physical frailness and lack of good health. That could be just as big a thorn in someone's life as the others. It's been said he could not see to write very well. Considering one of his giftings was writing letters that could be a real thorn in someone's side. We don't really know what it was, but we do know it was something that was near and dear to his heart. It was something he had to live with everyday.

People who make great strides in the Kingdom, like Paul, usually have great pain. They have great sorrow in their lives. They are pushed beyond what they think they are able or capable of doing. They have to totally trust God in their disappointments of life.

> "Jesus said, 'He who loves father or mother more than Me is not worthy of Me. And he who loves son or daughter more than Me is not worthy of Me.'"

> "He who finds his life will lose it! But he who loses his life for My sake will find it!'" Matthew 10:37-39.

Some people would say, "Oh that's so hard. How could He ask such a thing of us? I thought He was a God of love!"

Wake up!

He is the God of love! How quickly you forget what He did for you. How quickly you forget where you came from. Be thankful! You are not going to hell for all of eternity! He has revealed Himself to you, and now you have a real and meaningful relationship with the King of Glory, Jesus. This life has meaning now. It was nothing before without Him. His love for you is AMAZING!

> "He (the Lord of Glory) was led as a sheep to the slaughter; And as a lamb before its shearer is silent, So He opened not His mouth. In His humiliation His justice was taken away, And who will declare His generation? For His life is taken from the earth."
> Acts 8:32-33

Will you declare His generation? Will you pursue the King of the Kingdom? Are you running this race to receive the prize? The prize is the King! Not what this world has to offer.

> "LET THIS MIND BE IN YOU! which was also in Christ Jesus, who, being in the form of God, did not consider it robbery to be equal with God. But made Himself of no reputation, taking the form of a bondservant, and coming in the likeness of men. And being found in appearance as a man, HE (the Lord of Glory) HUMBLED

HIMSELF AND BECAME OBEDIENT TO
THE POINT OF DEATH, EVEN THE DEATH
OF THE CROSS." Philippians 2:5-8.

Life is not easy. I heard a very well-respected man
of God say once, "It seems the greater the call, the greater
the brokenness." It would seem that those who carry a
strong anointing have great brokenness in their lives before
God. Some could be self-inflicted from their pasts, some are
situations too painful to imagine.

> "The eyes of the Lord are toward the
> (uncompromisingly) righteous and His ears are
> open to their cry. The face of the Lord is against
> those who do evil, to cut off the remembrance of
> them from the earth. When the righteous cry for
> help, the Lord hears, and delivers them out of all
> their distress and troubles. The Lord is close to
> those who are of a broken heart and saves such as
> are crushed with sorrow for sin and are humbly
> and thoroughly penitent."
> Psalm 34:15-18 (AMP).

> "The sacrifices of God are a broken spirit, A
> broken and contrite heart—These, O God, You
> will not despise." Psalm 51:17 (AMP).

It just goes to show you that no one is exempt from pain. Whether it's self-inflicted or not, whether it's physical or mental, your heart and your soul have to deal with life. BUT GOD IS FAITHFUL! He has not only sent His Son to make a way for us, but He has given us the gift of His Helper, the Holy Spirit and His Anointing.

And that is why the Anointing is so much stronger on some people; they carry things we are unaware of. Don't be so quick to judge others. You don't know what they carry. And the reality is you really don't want to carry what they carry.

Remember, the Kingdom of God is about the King. If you will follow and be in relationship with Him, the answers you seek, He will give. Sometimes, the answers are not what we expected, but He will lead you and guide you into all truth.

> "His Lord said to him, 'Well done, good and faithful servant; You were FAITHFUL (you worked and labored for Me) over a few things (that I had given you), (so now) I (God) will MAKE YOU RULER OVER MANY THINGS. Enter into the Joy of your Lord!"

Chapter 7

HOW DOES YOUR ANOINTING GROW

Your relationship with the Holy Spirit is everything. He is God Almighty's presence living in you!

It still amazes me when I think that God, the Creator of all life, drew me in, and revealed Himself to me. I could be like so many people who don't give Him the time of day, or are even aware that He is there. He had mercy on me, and He had mercy on you, too. He revealed Himself to us! We have so much to be thankful for!

His presence, His inspiration, His empowerment is everything. Spending time with Him is the most important thing you can do with your life. It's something you have to take the time to do, and do it.

Can you help the Anointing of the Holy Spirit to grow in your life? Is there a real tangible way to help your personal Anointing to grow? Yes, there is.

How can I be so bold? It's because I have a real and

meaningful relationship with the Holy Spirit. I also have a real and meaningful relationship with Jesus. And believe it or not, God the Father is right there on the scene with me through Jesus and the Holy Spirit. It thrills my heart! It is the most amazing thing to walk with them! They are so very real, and it's no wonder there are so many distractions to keep you from Them.

This book is your opportunity to grow in the Anointing, to grow in your relationship with the Holy Spirit and Jesus.

There are three real tangible ways your personal Anointing will grow.

1. Your Anointing will grow through your relationship with the Holy Spirit; after all, He is the Anointing.
2. Your Anointing will grow by dedicating and yielding your gifts, talents, and abilities to Him, the presence of the Holy Spirit.
3. Your Anointing will grow by giving Him honor and being respectful of His presence. Respect is big when it comes to God. It is the beginning of true wisdom, and He expects it.

So, let's take a look at these three individually.

1. Your Anointing will grow through your relationship with the Holy Spirit.

Where, when, and how do you spend time with the Holy Spirit? The first place should be in your secret place of prayer, before you begin your day.

In Matthew 6:5-13 and in Luke 11:1-13, we have two different accounts of what we call 'The Lord's Prayer.' This is where Jesus said, "Thy Kingdom come, Thy will be done, On Earth as it is in Heaven." What is He talking about? He is talking about His Kingdom! The Kingdom of God Almighty, who sits on His throne in Heaven, watching over everything! HIS Kingdom on the Earth as it is in Heaven!

Where is His Kingdom on the Earth? It is in us! Where was it then? It was in the followers and believers of Jesus, who had experienced His touch in their lives.

Jesus wants His Kingdom on the Earth to exist as it is in Heaven THROUGH US! There is no other way. That is what He wanted then, and that is what He wants today.

This is not unattainable! He is very real and very attainable!

In the Book of Matthew it reads:

"And when you pray, you shall not be like the hypocrites. For they love to pray standing in the synagogues and on the corners of the streets, that they may be seen by men. Assuredly, I say to you, they have their reward. But you, when you pray, go into your room, and when you have shut your door, pray to your Father who is in the secret place; and your Father who sees in secret will reward you openly. And when you pray, do not use vain repetitions as the heathen do. For they think that they will be heard for their many words."

He, God, is listening for your heart to speak to His heart. Prayer needs to be heart-to-heart.

"Therefore, do not be like them. For your Father knows the things you have need of before you ask Him. In this manner, therefore, pray:
"Our Father in Heaven,
Hallowed be Your Name.
Your Kingdom come,
Your will be done
On earth as it is in Heaven.
Give us this day our daily bread,
And forgive us our debts,
As we forgive our debtors.
And do not lead us into temptation,
But deliver us from the evil one.
For Yours is the Kingdom
and the Power
and the Glory forever.
Amen."

Jesus talks about not being like the hypocrites who pray openly for all to hear. They were praying to be seen by man, not by God. There is no doubt about it, they got their reward. They were praying with soul power, not under the inspiration of the Holy Spirit and mainly not from their hearts. If they had been praying from their hearts, it would have had God's attention, which is His presence. God always hears prayers from the heart.

Consequently, their reward was all about themselves, not God. Because of their pride in their religion and traditions, their hearts were not open to seeing or hearing the truth of Who it was Who was standing right in front of them, the Son of God.

Jesus said to pray in your secret place, your private room, where it is only you and God. And then "your Father, Who sees in secret, will reward you openly."

Why would He want you to do that? Why would He want you to spend time with Him in secret? Because in the secret place God will reveal Himself to you! Your friendship and your relationship with God will grow there. You will learn His voice and His leading, you will receive answers where there were none, you will receive His peace in the midst of your storms and trials, and the assurance that He is with you, and it is there that your Anointing will grow! Those are really good reasons, if you ask me.

Here are some examples from the Bible that prove this point.

"Adam walked with God in the cool of the day." Genesis 3:8.

"And Enoch walked with God, and he was not, for God took him." Genesis 5:24.

"Noah found grace in the eyes of the Lord." Genesis 6:8.

"The Lord said to Abraham …" Genesis 12:1.

These men walked with God. They had a friendship with God. God made us for the express purpose of being in relationship with Him.

I could go on-and-on. Look at Jacob. He wanted God's blessing and took it! Genesis 25:29-34. He wrestled with the Angel of the Lord, and would not let go until he got it! Genesis 32:22-32. He had a relationship with God and followed His leading. God must have loved Jacob's determination to have His favor. In return, God watched over him and helped him all the days of his life.

And, of course, there is Moses and the prophets. Over and over again, God reaches out to us, trying to help us find our way to Him.

> "Here is what Jesus said, 'For only I, the Son of Man, have come to Earth, and will return to Heaven again. And as Moses lifted up the bronze snake on a pole in the wilderness, so I, the Son of Man, must be lifted up on a pole. So that everyone who believes in Me will have eternal life. For God so loved the world He gave His only Son, so that everyone who believes in Him will not perish, but have eternal life. God did not send His Son into the world to condemn it, but to save it!" John 3:14-17 NLT.

Just think about it, God Almighty, the Creator, wants one-on-one alone time with you! That is amazing! He wants you to know Him, because He already knows you!

Jesus is talking about building your relationship with God in your secret place.

Let me tell you something that a lot of people don't know. I would venture to say that only the remnant knows this. WHEN YOU GO TO YOUR SECRET PLACE OF PRAYER AND GIVE HONOR AND RESPCT TO THE HOLY SPIRIT—AND YOU YIELD TO THE HOLY SPIRIT

THERE—YOUR ANOINTING (THE MANIFESTED PRESENCE OF GOD) WILL GROW IN YOUR LIFE!

When you put God first in your life by spending time with Him first, it shows Him that you respect Him. And that is what establishes God's Kingdom on the Earth as it is in Heaven. YOU! You establish God's Kingdom on the Earth as it is in Heaven by yielding to Who the Holy Spirit is. It's not complicated.

Let me tell you how.

First, of all, when you go there, you must acknowledge Him. You talk to Him. You tell Him how much you love Him and how thankful you are to have Him in your life. Allow Him to be your best friend, that's what He wants.

Secondly, ask Him to lead you in your prayer time and then yield to Him, the Holy Spirit. It's something you have to practice. It's like going into another dimension—the God realm. His presence and Anointing will lead you, teach you, and give you insight and understanding. There is nothing like it. Once you have learned how to yield to the Holy Spirit in your secret place, you can yield to Him anywhere and at anytime. You can tap into the Anointing whenever and wherever you need His help.

He will give you what you need. Let Him fill you and your room, your secret place with His presence and ask Him to take over your life. He only has good plans for you.

When you do that, everything will change. Your prayer time will become the most wonderful time of the day, and you will look forward to it. Being in the presence of the Holy Spirit is awesome. There is nothing like it. His love, His peace, His inspiration is absolutely the most powerful thing that could ever happen to your life! Honor and show respect to the Holy Spirit in your secret place of prayer and learn how to yield to Him.

Now then, let's look in the Book of Luke and see how it reads:

> "Now it came to pass He was praying in a
> certain place, when He ceased (from praying)
> one of His disciples said to Him, 'Lord, teach
> us to pray, as John also taught his disciples.'
> So, He, (Jesus) said to them,
> 'When you pray, say:
> 'Our Father in Heaven,
> Hallowed be Your Name.
> Your Kingdom come,
> Your will be done
> On earth as it is in Heaven.
> Give us day by day our daily bread,
> And forgive us our sins,
> For we also forgive everyone who is indebted to us,
> And do not lead us into temptation,
> But deliver us from the evil one.'"

"And then He asked them, 'Which of you shall have a friend, and go to him at midnight and say to him, 'Friend lend me three loaves, for a friend of mine has come to me on his journey, and I have nothing to set before him;' and he will answer from within and say, 'Do not trouble me; the door is now shut, and my children are with me in bed; I cannot rise and give to you;' I say to you, though he will not rise and give to him because he is his friend, yet because of his persistence he will rise and give him as many as he needs. So I say to you, 'ask, and it will be given to you; seek, and you will find; knock, and it will be opened to you. For everyone who asks receives, and he who seeks finds, and to him who knocks it will be opened. If a son asks for bread from any father among you, will he give him a stone? Or if he asks for a fish, will he give him a serpent instead of a fish? Or if he asks for an egg, will he offer him a scorpion? If you then, being evil, know how to give good gifts to your children, how much more will your Heavenly Father give the Holy Spirit to those who ask Him!'" Luke 11:1-13

Here Jesus is teaching His disciples how to pray and how to receive the Holy Spirit! Why would He teach those together? It's because your relationship with the Holy Spirit and your relationship with God in prayer are the same. They are like a hand in a glove. Yes, they are two different individuals, but very much one Spirit.

You need the inspiration of the Holy Spirit for your prayer life and for your Anointing to grow. The Holy Spirit is the Anointing. The Holy Spirit is Who God the Father uses to lead you and guide you. The more quality time you spend with Him in prayer and in the secret place, the easier it is to yield and to follow Him. They all flow and work together: the Holy Spirit in relationship, the Holy Spirit in the Anointing, and the Holy Spirit in prayer.

Your gifts and talents without the Anointing is what the world has to offer, but your gifts and talents with the Anointing is SUPERNATURAL. It's beyond this realm. It's God's realm. The Anointing gives you the ability to live in God's realm. It's God the Father's gift to you. It's beyond the world's reach. All they have is soul power, but you, YOU! have the Anointing, the powerful presence of God Almighty! And nothing can compare.

2. If you want your Anointing to grow you must dedicate and yield your gifts, talents and abilities to Him.

As you grow each day in your relationship with the Holy Spirit in your secret place and in everyday life, ask Him to bless your gifts and talents. We just read where Jesus said, "Ask and you will receive." So, ask Him to bless your gifts and talents, and they will be blessed. Ask Him to cause them to grow and multiply in the Anointing, and they will grow and multiply in the influence of the Anointing, His inspiration!

When you speak out loud with your voice, the ripple effects of the vibration in the Spirit realm, spirit-to-Spirit, heart-to-Heart, sends waves from your heart and your spirit to His. That is why prayers and worship are so powerful with music. The stronger the waves you make in the spiritual realm or atmosphere, the stronger the Anointing will flow and grow in your personal life.

This doesn't mean you are to yell when you pray; it means you pray with your heart and yield to the Anointing. This is what determines the dynamics of your prayers. It doesn't mean the music needs to be loud, either. Music not only stirs our emotions, but it stirs the whole dynamo of the spirit realm, as well.

The Anointing can flow in many ways: in revelation, understanding, answers where there seem to be none, hope, an unmoving faith, knowledge of His Word and how it applies to where you are right now, and the wisdom to know what to do or what to say in the situations life seems to throw us into.

Give your gifts and talents to Him as an offering of worship. Worship Him in your gifts and talents. It is an offering acceptable for Him.

If your gift is helps … when you go to help someone, do it as worship to God. If your gift is in finances … give or administer those finances as worship to God. Whichever and whatever gift or talent you have, do it as a form of worship to God. It is given heart-to-Heart, spirit-to-Spirit. He has given you something to sow, so sow it! And let God bring the increase!

Here is an example of what I'm talking about. I'd like to share my testimony with you. When I was a little girl, I'm talking a young girl, about four or five years old, I loved to sing to the Lord when I went to bed at night. Sweet, huh? But we lived in a house with thin walls and everyone could hear me. So my mother would yell at me from down the hall to be quiet and to go to sleep. Of course, she said it sweetly, but sternly. But because I was so determined in my heart to give my little love songs to Jesus, I would hang my head over the side of my bed and as softly as I could, I would sing to the Lord.

It all started there. I was a worshiper. I was called by the gift He had given me. It was the gift of music, and the song of the Lord that was in me was naturally coming out. I didn't know what I was doing. I just loved doing it and doing it for Him.

When I was in grade school, I wanted to be in the band because I didn't want to do P.E. I was very small and fragile. I wanted to play the trombone which was twice the size of me. My Dad wanted me to play the drums, because he thought it would make me popular. My sister wanted me to play the sax, because it was a cool instrument. The band director wanted me to play the French horn. But my Mom wanted me to play the flute, because we already had one from when my sister was in band. So, I played the flute from the fifth grade to my senior year in high school. Little did I know that God was directing my life.

After I graduated from High School, I, like so many of us, did not have a clue about what I wanted to do with my life. I enjoyed my flute while in school, but I really enjoyed being a part of the band more than anything else. I kind of wanted to do something with it, but didn't see a real future for me in it. I was not ready to make long-term decisions and was pushed off into college like my two sisters with an associate of business, which was in secretarial skills.

The song of the Lord was in my heart, even though I didn't know what it was. I could feel it.

A few years later, I got filled with the Holy Spirit. When that happened, I began to ask God to lead me and guide me. I asked Him over and over for more and more of Him. I was singing in my little Holy Ghost church, but I wanted more of Him. And then He opened the door for me to go to Christ

For The Nations Bible School in Dallas, Texas. Immediately, I was inspired by the Holy Spirit to pick up my flute again. I really did not know why.

When I went to the tryouts for the band, I was told to go ahead and sing something in case I wanted to be in the choir. You had to try out for everything in order to be in it. I was the last one, because I was so shy and didn't know what to expect. There was just me, a student pianist and a student band leader. Everyone else had left for the day. So I closed my eyes to sing a song to the Lord. I think it was a hymn. I don't remember. When I opened my eyes there were five or six adults (teachers and professors) standing there smiling and applauding me. I was so-o-o embarrassed.

I was offered a position in their prestigious small group of traveling singers, called Living Praise. I was flabbergasted. I didn't know anything about Living Praise, what it was, or the school in general for that matter. I turned them down and joined the band. There, I learned how to flow in the Holy Spirit on my flute. I learned how to prophesy on it, and then, give the interpretations. The Holy Spirit would literally flow through me. It was amazing, and I still love it to this day!

I believe because I was obedient to pick up my flute the first year there, He allowed me to join the Living Praise Choir the next year and travel all over the United States and Canada. We were ministering almost every weekend and on Wednesday nights. Wow! What an incredible experience I will always cherish.

Now what I didn't tell you were the hours of worship I spent in my secret place of prayer—singing, worshiping, playing my flute, and of course, praying. All of it was led by the inspiration of the Holy Spirit. That was the place I went to early in the morning before school started, and in the afternoon after classes. I was there to grow and to give Him honor and respect with the gifts and Anointing He had given me. I was living in the secret place! How wonderful!

To this day I still do it. It's not only my gift, but it is my calling. It is my life. It is who I am. I pursued it in the secret place. I honored Him with it by dedicating and giving it to Him as worship. AND HE GAVE THE INCREASE WITH HIS ANOINTING!

I'd like to add this nugget. When I go to my secret place of prayer, I always start by inviting and asking the Holy Spirit to lead me in my prayer time. I ask for increase in His Anointing and for His Anointing to direct me. I always ask Him because He knows my future and He knows what I have need of. He sees the whole picture. He knows the ending before the beginning began!

Yes, there is truth to this old saying: use what you have or you will lose it. But there is also a choice we have in "how" we will use our gifts! Dedicate your gifts and talents to Him. Use what He has given you. Let Him direct your life. Follow the inspiration of the Holy Spirit. You may not see what He is doing until you are almost at the end of your journey. But remember this: God is faithful to bring increase. If you will dedicate your gifts and talents to the Anointing, He will cause it to increase.

3. If you want your Anointing to grow, you absolutely must give Him, the Anointing of the Holy Spirit, honor and to show respect in His presence.

How do you show respect in His presence? You yield to Him.

First of all, I have already talked to you about yielding to the Holy Spirit in your secret place of prayer and in the actual use of your gifts and talents. But now I'm talking about yielding to the Holy Spirit throughout the day and your life.

Show Him respect by being attentive to His leading. He may lead you to go somewhere you would not usually go to or even to go at a different time than you would normally go—all for a Divine appointment He has set up for you or to keep you safe from harm. You see, He is constantly working with us, and a lot of times, we are not even aware that it was Him working, until later! He will lead you in shopping for the best deal. He will nudge at you to eat properly. He will give you understanding and inspire you in your work. He will also lead you in your finances—where and when to give—so He can work in your finances for you. You must sow your seed in order to receive a crop.

The things that are important to us are important to Him. You'd be surprised at how much He wants to bless you and help you.

Now, let's talk about King David and Joseph. These are a couple of our favorite guys in the Bible. Even though not everyone is called to be a King or a leader, there is much to be said about their lives. Both of them were obviously led by God.

King David was a boy who was destined for greatness. Sadly, his family pretty much left him to himself. They obviously didn't think much of him. He spent his time as a shepherd in the fields, and through his love for God, he played his harp and sang songs to Him. He was ministering to God in His secret place! He was following and yielding to the inspiration of the Holy Spirit, the Anointing. He was practicing his sling shot, just in case another wild animal should show up. Of course, what young man wouldn't work on his sling shot skills? What an amazing beginning! Even though David was unaware, God was in the process of preparing him for greatness. The bear and the lion he killed, while he was protecting his father's flocks, was just the beginning.

At one time, King David really messed things up, even though he was a man after God's own heart. He had committed adultery, got the girl pregnant, had her husband killed to cover it up, but everyone found out about it anyway, and their baby died. Out of desperation he cried out, "Do not take your presence from me!"

Like I have said over and over again, the presence of the Holy Spirit and His Anointing is everything! Without Him, we can do nothing, and we are nothing without Him!

David knew how to use his gifts and talents while under the inspiration of the Holy Spirit's Anointing. He became a great psalmist and a great warrior. Today, everyone knows his story, both the good and the bad. It just goes to show you God's goodness and mercy. Even though sometimes he really missed the mark, God still forgave him and helped him. Why? Because David loved God! He had a relationship with God! And he showed God his love and zeal for Him through his songs and praise of Him. He brought the Ark of the Covenant back to the city of David, Jerusalem, with extravagant dance, praise, songs and sacrifices! David knew how to pour his love out to God!

Joseph was the eleventh son of twelve! You could say he was the low man on the totem pole. Nobody seemed to like him, and His Mom had died giving birth to his younger brother, so he had no one to lean on growing up. Even though he had a big family, I'm sure he felt very much alone like David. His dad, Jacob, somehow knew Joseph was the one God had chosen for greatness in the family. He tried to be attentive to that by teaching him all he knew about the family business. So between his dad's mentoring and his personal gifting, the Holy Spirit led him to be one of the greatest leaders ever known in history.

We need to have reverence and respect for God and follow the Holy Spirit. We need to allow Him to work in our lives. Even though at times, life can seem horrible, God is still with us. He is right there with us on the scene: leading, guiding, and helping.

Moses said it, too! "I do not want to go without you!"

Here was a guy, who was destined for greatness. He was known as the meekest man on the Earth; yet, he knew he was the "vessel" God had ordained to use. He knew it wasn't him working. It was God working through him. He learned to get alone with God. He learned His presence, and he learned obedience through his suffering.

Moses, just like David and just like Joseph, had to make his own way with God. All three of these men were "pushed" into their destiny, and they went with God's presence, the inspiration of the Holy Spirit's Anointing.

We can have that today. Jesus gave us His "Seal of Approval!"

Be open when you feel His leading. Don't ignore Him! We are the temple of the Holy Spirit! He is with us all the time. He is constantly leading and guiding us. We must try to be sensitive to Him and to keep ourselves aware of His leading.

The Holy Spirit is wonderful about inspiring us in our gifts and talents, because He gave them to us, and He wants to see us grow in them. He wants us to grow in His Anointing. Like I said earlier, your relationship with the Holy Spirit is everything.

As a result of His kindness and goodness toward us, we want to bless and express our love to the Holy Spirit, Jesus, and God the Father in our gifts and talents that He has so graciously given us. We want to show Him our gratefulness and thankfulness by yielding to His inspiration and leading. It is there that we will grow in our anointing. It is there that the Kingdom of God will be on the Earth as it is in Heaven. And it is there that our relationship with Him will flourish.

PRAYER:

"Holy Spirit, thank You for the gifts and talents You have given me. Inspire me and lead me with Your presence and Your Anointing. Encourage me and help me to follow Your leading. Bring increase to the Anointing You have given me. Flood me with Your Presence. Let me know You are always with me. You are so awesome and so good to me. I love You. Thank You so much.

"I will bless the Lord who has given me counsel;
My heart also instructs me in the night seasons.
I have set the Lord always before me;
Because He is at my right hand, I shall not be moved."
Psalm 16:7-8

Chapter 8

HOW TO
GUARD YOUR ANOINTNG

ABSOLUTE ONE—GOD IS GOOD!

The Scripture says:

> "They will make war with the Lamb (Jesus,
> our Redeemer and True High Priest), but the
> Lamb (Our Champion) will overcome them
> because He is LORD OF LORDS AND KING
> OF KINGS—and with Him will be His called,
> chosen and faithful followers." Revelation
> 17:14, (Emphasis added.)

I want to be one of His called, chosen and faithful
followers, and I know you do, too! But in order to do that
we must guard our relationship with Jesus and our friendship
with the Holy Spirit.

The called are those who simply answer the calling of God on their lives. They received Jesus, the One and only true Redeemer, as their personal Savior.

The chosen are those who went further in their walk with God and they received the baptism of the Holy Spirit, the Seal of Approval.

The faithful are those who are consistent in all of the above. They are consistent in their fellowship with the Word, Jesus. They are consistent in the secret place of prayer through their friendship of the Holy Spirit. They followed the instructions in the Word of God, Jesus, and the leading of the Holy Spirit, so much so, that they loved not their lives even unto the death.

Here they are again, the called, the chosen and the faithful in another passage.

> "And they overcame him by the blood of the Lamb, the word of their testimony and they loved not their lives unto the death."
> Revelation 12:11 (Emphasis added.)

They are the called, the chosen and the faithful.

> "And they (the called) overcame him (the devil) by the blood of the Lamb (by the blood of Jesus), (and the chosen went further and

they) overcame him (the devil) by the Word of their testimony (by the Anointing of the Holy Spirit), and (then the faithful, even went further and were not afraid to) overcome him (the devil) (to the point that) they did not love their lives to the death." (Emphasis added.)

Remember this? God has purpose, plans, callings, giftings, and destinies for you. He has things in His heart He has prepared for you, not only in this life, but in the life to come. How wonderful is that?

It's all about God's Kingdom. It's all about serving the King of the Kingdom, and that is Jesus.

This life is not all a bowl of cherries, but in Jesus, and in the friendship of His Holy Spirit, there is peace, joy, and love beyond measure. He will help us each step of the way.

When Paul wrote this letter to Timothy, He had been brought back to prison a second time in Rome under Nero, and he wrote.

"So do not be ashamed to testify about our Lord, or ashamed of me His prisoner. But join with me in suffering for the gospel, by the power of God, who has saved us and called us to a holy life—not because of anything we have done but because of His own purpose

and grace. This grace was given us in Christ Jesus before the beginning of time, but it has now been revealed through the appearing of our Savior, Christ Jesus, who has destroyed death and has brought life and immortality to light through the gospel. And of this gospel I was appointed a herald and an apostle and a teacher. That is why I am suffering as I am. Yet I am not ashamed, because I know whom I have believed, and am convinced that He is able to guard what I have entrusted to Him for that day. What you heard from me, keep as the pattern of sound teaching, with faith and love in Christ Jesus. Guard the good deposit that was entrusted to you—guard it with the help of the Holy Spirit who lives in us."
2 Timothy 1:8-14.

Paul was very clear about guarding the good deposit that was entrusted to you and to not be ashamed of what God has done for you. Over and over again, I have talked to you about the cost of the blood of Jesus for your salvation. I have talked to you about the baptism of the Holy Spirit and His precious friendship. I have talked to you about living a life without sin, so that the power of the Anointing would be great in you. God has deposited His very presence in you.

So, in order to guard your Anointing there are three absolutes you really need to know. They will give you confidence and strengthen your faith in Who He is and what He is doing.

ABSOLUTE ONE—GOD IS GOOD!

God created all the stars and the galaxies, and all that goes on out there in space, with us in His heart and on His mind. That, in and of itself, is so incredible! He knows exactly what He is doing. He thought it all through before He started. He knew the end from before He started the beginning.

He is so perfect in what He does, and yes, He is so very obvious. If you have eyes to see Him, you can see Him in everything.

Our very own scientists have discovered everything, that is all of life and everything that exists, is based off of two sound waves. Sound waves! The smallest piece of the atom goes all the way down to two sound waves.

Let's read about how God created life in Genesis 1:1-3, (Emphasis added.)

"In the beginning God created the heavens and the earth. The earth was without form and an empty waste, and darkness was upon the face of the very great deep. The Spirit of God (the

Holy Spirit) was moving over the face of the waters, AND GOD SAID, Let there be …"

Now let's look at how the Apostle John describes it in: John 1:1-3, (Emphasis added.)

"In the beginning (before all time) was the Word (Christ), and the Word (Jesus Christ) was with God, and the Word was God Himself (the Word is God's Son, who is one with God). He (Jesus the Christ) was present originally with God. All things were made and came into existence through Him; and without Him was not even one thing made that has come into being."

In the Old and New Testaments, God spoke, and His sound waves created everything. It is God the Father and God the Son, the two sound waves, in perfect harmony together in life and creation! Those who have eyes to see can see God the Father and God the Son in all of creation and life.

Those who are bent on believing that God does not exist, quickly try to keep the world from knowing about these scientific proofs that He does exist. However, it was too late on this one; Christians all over the world quickly caught wind of it.

God IS smarter than us, and He IS good!

For example, our solar system was created to function in perfect total harmony. He specifically created Planet Earth for us to live on, in this solar system. He made it for us. Just think of all the different kinds of life there are here. He surrounded us with all of His different facets of beauty and sound and life. But wait; that's not all! He has given us the ability to experience it all! We can see it. We can hear it. We can smell it. We can taste it. We can touch it. And we can even feel it in our souls!

God is so awesome, and He is so-o-o good!

God has done all that just for us! Not the devil and all his fallen demons. It's for us! He really loves us! He really is good!

There is a big picture here. A much bigger picture than we can fathom. It's eternity. This life, this beginning, is so small in comparison to eternity. He has something so much bigger for us than what we have here in this life. He wants us to believe Him now, so He can bless us then, too. He wants us to be in fellowship with Him now, because we will be in fellowship with Him then, as well. Our future is in eternity, and our eternity is in Him!

What can we do to help others find Him? How can we help others find Him? I'll tell you straight up! By our daily fellowship in the Word of God and our daily fellowship with the Holy Spirit! It's that simple. As we pray, as we read, and as we listen and obey the voice of the Holy Spirit and His leading, then the Kingdom of God will grow and flourish. The Holy Spirit leads us and helps us with only what the Lord Jesus tells Him to do and say. The Lord Jesus tells the Holy Spirit only what the Father God tells Him to say. There is no wondering if something is of God or not, when you know Him and His voice.

God loves you so much, even before the beginning of time, that He gave His only Son, Jesus, for you. You see, God the Father, God the Son, and God the Holy Spirit had a plan before they began the beginning. They made a way for you to be bought back from the enemy of your soul, the devil.

God is good! God gave Jesus up as a sacrifice for your life. Jesus went, of His own free will, in your place and took the penalty for your sins. The suffering He went through was for you. He paid the price for your sins. So, when you asked Him to forgive you of your sins, you received His free gift of salvation, because He paid for it. He is the only One Who can give you life eternal. He is the only One Who has paid the price for your sins.

The All-Knowing, All-Perfect, All-Present God has done all of this for you, because He loves you. And because He is good!

Then, after Jesus was resurrected from the dead and ascended into Heaven, He sent you His gift of the Holy Spirit. The fellowship of the Holy Spirit's Anointing that lives in you is God the Father's Seal of Approval for you. He approved of you when you received His Son's sacrifice for you. The Seal or the Gift of the Holy Spirit is the fellowship of the Anointing which is God's manifested presence living in you.

God is good!

Your personal Anointing is your giftings, talents, and abilities that He has uniquely given to you in your very own DNA. It is for your calling, and you are called to be in fellowship with the Holy Spirit's Anointing. This means, God is good!

Of all the other things and so called gods out there that people serve, none have ever done anything for anyone. None of them love you. None of them give you peace of mind. None of them can give you eternal life!

God is good!

He is the only One Who can give you eternal life. THERE ARE NOT many roads to salvation. As a matter of fact, there are NO OTHER ROADS to salvation. There is only one way, through Jesus Christ, the Son of the Living God. He is the only One Who died for your sins. He is the only One Who can forgive you of your sins. And He is the only way to bring you to God the Father and to have a valid experience with God the Father.

In order to guard your Anointing, you need to know that God is good. No matter what happens, God is good. No matter where you go, God is good. He is faithful. He is for you. And He is good!

"For God knew His people in advance (before He began the beginning He knew you), and He chose them to become like His Son (He chose you before you were born to be in relationship with Him through His Son, and to be like His Son), so that His Son would be the firstborn, with many brothers and sisters (that's you). And having chosen them, He called them to come to Him (Because He loves you so much He chose you, and He called you to come to Him). And He gave them right standing with Himself (and He gave you right standing with Himself through His Son, Jesus), and He promised them His glory (He has promised you eternal life with Him in the glorious place He lives, in the place of His presence). What can we say about such wonderful things as these? (God is Good!) If God is for us, who can ever be against us? Since God did not spare even His own Son but gave Him up for us all, won't God, who gave us Christ, also give us everything? (Won't God, who gave us Christ Jesus also give us His seal of approval, the fellowship of the Holy Spirit anointing?) Can anything ever separate us from Christ's love? (Can anything ever separate you from the fact that Jesus loves you so much He laid down His life for you?) Does it mean He no longer loves us if we have trouble or calamity, or are persecuted, or are hungry or cold or in danger or threatened with death? (NO! If anything, it means that He loves you even the more!) Even the scriptures say, 'For your sake we are killed every day; we are being slaughtered like sheep.' No! Despite all these things, the overwhelming victory is ours through Christ! Who loved us!

I AM CONVENCED! THAT NOTHING CAN EVER SEPARATE US FROM HIS LOVE!" Romans 8:29-32, 35-38 (NLV, Emphasis added.)

GOD IS GOOD!!!

In order to guard your Anointing you need to know that God is good. No matter what happens, God is good. No matter where you go, God is good. He is faithful. He is for you. And He is good!

He chose you before the beginning of time. And then He created the stars, this solar system, this planet and all the life and beauty there is here FOR YOU. Jesus came of His own free will FOR YOU and gave His life FOR YOU. And then when you were finally born on this Earth, the Holy Spirit was working and drawing you in. His goodness and His mercies are from everlasting to everlasting.

In order to guard your anointing you must absolutely know that GOD IS GOOD! No matter what happens, God is good!

Chapter 9

HOW TO
GUARD YOUR ANOINTING

ABSOLUTE TWO—
KNOW YOUR SEASON

"Now it came to pass in the 13th year, in the 4th month, on the 5th day of the month, as I was among the captives by the River Chebar, that the Heavens were opened and I saw visions of God." Ezekiel 1:1.

At the beginning of Ezekiel, and many other places in the Bible, you will notice there are specific days and seasons of events that took place. They are noted there for a reason.

There are different seasons for different times of our lives. First of all, there is the chronological time God has set up for us to live in, which is the years, the months, days, hours and so on. He has put the stars in the Heavens and the planets in their place as signs for us to know the times and the seasons we are living in.

For example: There are natural seasons we live in.

Spring: Spring is when you plant your seeds. It is a time of digging up the ground to prepare the soil. You feed it with the right nutrients the seeds need to help it grow and produce.

Summer: Summer is a time when you watch over your seed. You make sure your ground does not get too dry. You keep it watered, and sometimes, you feed it with fertilizer. You watch over your crop to make sure it grows in a healthy environment. You also don't want any varmints or small animals getting into your crops. And you want to make sure your neighbors cattle don't go trampling through it, either. So, in the summer you protect your crop!

Fall: Fall is the season you harvest what you have planted in the spring and watched over during the summer. Harvest is work. You have to get out there and bring it in yourself. You can't just sit back like the grasshopper did and do nothing. Usually, you can get pretty dirty doing it, too. It is also a time of setting aside some seed for the spring again. You don't want to eat your seed during the winter. You want to always set aside the best part of your harvest to plant in the spring, so you can have the best possible harvest. And the fall is a time of being thankful and sharing your blessings with others.

Winter: Winter is a season of rest. You rest the ground from all of its labor. You let it get rejuvenated. I used to pray over my children when they were little that their sleep would be sweet and peaceful, that the Holy Spirit would have sweet communion with their spirits as they slept, that He would hover over them and love on them while they slept, and that when they woke up they would be refreshed, happy and healthy. So, the winter is very much needed. You need that rest. It is a time of resting your ground from its labor.

Now, let's look again at verses 2-3:

"On the 5th day of the month, which was in the 5th year of King Jehoiachin's captivity, The word of the Lord came expressly to Ezekiel the priest, the son of Buzi, in the land of the Chaldeans by the River Chebar, and the hand of the Lord was upon him there."

Here the Lord repeats Himself, telling us of a specific time and season. He starts with the day, and goes to the month, and then goes to the year. And He even tells you the season the people were living in.

Stay with me; I'm going somewhere with this.

So, let's start with the day: How does our day begin? With the spring! Oh! Have we heard this before? First thing in the morning we spend time with our Lord in our secret place and there He sows in us. He sows His presence, His Word, His insight, and His instructions for the day in us.

This is when and where we receive our encouragement, our strength, and our answers to the situations we are in. His Anointing, the Holy Spirit, is there for us. He is the Helper. He knows what we need and is ready to give it to us. He wants to cultivate your ground, or prepare your soul for the day with His presence and His Anointing. He wants to sow in your mind and your thoughts His Word, His knowledge and His wisdom for you to grow in throughout your day.

Second, there is the summer of your day. This is when you take what He gave you in your Secret Place that morning and you use it. Now, you are meditating, cultivating, and watching over what was sown in your heart that morning. You are growing and applying it to your life.

Next, comes the fall of your day. At the end of your day you prepare for rest. You enjoy a good meal and relax. You reflect on your day. You take what He gave you that morning and you thank Him for it. You have a grateful heart for His leading you, and guiding you, and being with you throughout your day.

Then, last, but by no means least, there is the winter of your day, where you rest from all your labors throughout the day. You sleep. Your body, your soul, and even your spirit need to rest.

Now considering your day let's read Psalm 16:5-9.

> "O Lord, You are the portion of my inheritance
> and my cup;
> You maintain my lot.
> The lines have fallen to me in pleasant places;
> Yes, I have a good inheritance.
> I will bless the Lord who has given me counsel;
> My heart also instructs me in the night seasons.
> I have set the Lord always before me;
> Because He is at my right hand I shall not be
> moved.
> Therefore my heart is glad, and my glory rejoices;
> My flesh also will rest in hope."

Now let's talk about the month.

The month is a chronological time of about 30 days. Why is that important? It takes an overall group of days that were in a "specific season" of the year for you to look at. What was happening during that month of that season of the year? What was so significant about it?

Let's read it again.

> "Now it came to pass in the 13th year, in the 4th
> month on the 5th day of the month …"

We know that according to the Jewish calendar the 4th month of the year is Tammuz. It has 29 days and is during the middle of our time of June to July.

So this vision Ezekiel had, happened and was written in the season of summer. During this season, it's just getting started to be really hot. It would be a time to watch your crop and keep it watered. August is coming, and you know how hot August is. You don't want your crop to burn up in August, so you have to keep a watch over it. You want it to really get to growing good and healthy. Make sure you have a good fence to keep cattle out and set traps for small animals that would try to eat your crop. Summer is a time when there is growth. It is a time when there is heat.

There are visions and dreams God gives us, and just when it's really starting to grow, things happen, people say things and the pressure is on. Did I really hear from God? Was that really real? The enemy would have loved to have stolen Ezekiel's experience and vision from him, but thank God he did not.

It would seem in the difficult times of our lives is where there is real growth. Where there is pressure, what's the old saying? "It separates the men from the boys."

Growing is work. Feeding your family, taking care of your home, just maintaining the basics of life—is work.

"He knows we have need of these things, but if you will seek FIRST the Kingdom of God and His righteousness! (Aha!) He will make sure that all those things will be taken care of for you." Matthew 6:33. (Emphasis added.)

So, you must start your day with Him! Seek Him first. Being in fellowship with Him will make it all happen! It will all come together. "He will work all things together for you good!" Romans 8:28.

But it is work! You must walk in obedience to His leading. If you don't do it, who will? If you don't stand in the gap for your family and loved ones, who will? If you don't pray for the world crisis, who will? If you don't know what to do—do the last thing He told you to do! Follow His instructions. We all fit together like a puzzle. When everyone does their part, it all comes together, and it works.

If we are in the Season of Summer, and I believe we are, it is time to watch over your crop!

Considering your Month and Season let's read this:
"Trust in the Lord with all your hearts,
And lean not on your own understanding;
In all your ways acknowledge Him,
(and what will He do?)

And He will direct your paths.
Do not be wise in your own eyes;
Fear the Lord and depart from evil!
It will be health to your flesh,
And strength to your bones."
Proverbs 3:5-8. (Emphasis added.)

Now let's read this again; the whole thing together.

"Now it came to pass in the 13th year, in the 4th month on the 5th day of the month, as I was among the captives by the River Chebar, that the heavens were opened and I saw visions of God. Now it came to pass in the 13th year, in the 4th month, on the 5th day of the month, which was in the 5th year of King Jehoiachin's captivity, ..." Ezekiel 1:1-3.

The Year: The date of the year was given during the reign of the King Jehoiachin. He was 18 years old when He became King and reigned for only three months.

When I was doing my research about this season in Israel's life, I thought they were an independent nation that had gone astray from serving God, but at this time, King Jehoiachin was merely King Nebuchadnezzar's governor, and they were already on their last leg of independence. The nation had pushed their limit with God, and God was using Nebuchadnezzar to punish His people. After three months as king, Jehoiachin rebelled against Nebuchadnezzar.

So, Nebuchadnezzar invaded Judah and took Jerusalem for himself.

Now you have to realize what state Israel was in at this time. It is clear. Solomon was a wise man, but he also had a downfall. As most men do, he liked women. So he married women from all over the world to make peace with their countries. But in so doing, he allowed all of them to build and continue their worship of idols.

While Solomon's son was king, he totally walked away from Jehovah God, and bad went to worse. King after king turned further and further away from the One true Jehovah God and worshiped idols. There were a couple of kings here and there who walked with God and things were good, but it was only for their season.

That is until Manasseh became king. Jehovah God had had all He could take. It was bad enough that the kings had been leading the people to worship idols, but now they were sacrificing their own babies to demon gods! Their cup was full.

There was a lot going on at this time. There were prophets all over the place proclaiming the truth of Jehovah God's anger, but no one was listening. No one wanted to hear the truth. As Jesus said, "people love darkness rather than light, because their deeds were evil." John 3:19.

This was the time of Jeremiah, Daniel, Ezekiel, Obadiah and Habakkuk. There is something very significant about this time and season in Israel's life. God had all these men living and experiencing His will and His desires. They were faithful men recording it for Israel and us, the remnant, even for today.

Jeremiah was King Josiah's prophet and confidant, and he saw a revival during his reign. Quickly after Josiah's death, Jeremiah suffered rounds of great persecution and horrific imprisonment, because of his stand for righteousness. Without righteousness the judgment of God was coming.

Righteousness is being in right-standing with God. The nation, under the rule of Manasseh, was not in right-standing with God, to say the least.

Obadiah also warned the people of God's judgment and the destruction of Jerusalem, but there is not much known about him personally.

Habakkuk's book is a conversation he is having with God. He is complaining to God of how the leaders are oppressing the poor. God answers him and assures him that He will punish them. God tells him how He is going to do it, through the wicked Chaldeans. Habakkuk doesn't like the idea of the wicked being used to bring judgment on God's chosen people, but God answers him, "The just shall live by faith."

From what I could tell, Jehoiachin was the 17th king after Solomon. Jeremiah warned Jehoiachin not to rebel against Nebuchadnezzar, but he did it anyway, and King Nebuchadnezzar invaded Jerusalem.

King Nebuchadnezzar took Jerusalem from King Jehoiachin and his family, who quickly surrendered in just a few hours. He took everyone captive and carried them all away to exile in Babylon. This is the group Daniel and his friends were in. Only the poorest people of the land were left.

Nebuchadnezzar took everyone and everything. He stole everything out of the temple for himself as his own personal spoils, and then, he destroyed the temple.

The reference to the 13th year is clearly a note to the season Ezekiel was living in. It was five years after Jehoiachin had surrendered, and the whole city of Jerusalem had been taken into captivity. Five years is a long time. Ezekiel was living with the captives by the River Chebar. There they were, five years in exile, separated from their homes and everything they had and loved. It was also when God called Ezekiel to be a prophet to the nation with his first vision. This first vision spanned the time of seven days! Can you imagine having a vision from God that lasted a week? Amazing!

Ezekiel spent the rest of his life and ministry in Babylon in exile. Does that mean God was not faithful to Ezekiel? Of course not! God was and is faithful to all who call upon the Name of the Lord, to all who believe Him, to all who love Him. But this life is not dedicated to having fun and being carefree. It's dedicated to fulfilling the will of God for our lives. Shall the pot ask the potter, "What are you doing?" As if to imply, "You don't know what you are doing!" or "You're doing it the wrong way!" Isaiah 45:5-10.

The high calling of God on a life is what God chooses. We need to stay strong and be true to Him. His ways are higher than ours, His thoughts are definitely higher than ours, and the times and the seasons we live in are by His choosing. Job 11:7-9; Isaiah 55:8-9.

We need to put Him first, and keep Him first.

And so now we know the year or season of Ezekiel's vision. It was during a time when the people of God were in exile for turning away from their Beloved Jehovah. They were all caught up in the world they were living in—doing their own thing. Following after what "they" thought was right and leaving God out of their decisions, a scary thought for the remnant, but very real.

In these last days, Jesus said if He did not shorten the days that even His elect would fall, because of the deception of the wicked one. The problem with deception is that you don't know you are deceived, that is what deception is.

That is why we need the Holy Spirit to draw us to Jesus and reveal Him to us. We need Him to keep us in the light, so we don't fall into deception and darkness. We also need Jesus and His written Word to keep us on the straight and narrow. It is so important for us to know that the deception in these last days will be so rampant, and it will be right in your face, just like it was in the days of Sodom and Gomorrah.

> "Jesus said, 'And unless those days were shortened, no flesh would be saved; but for the elect's sake those days will be shortened. Then if anyone says to you, Look, here is the Christ! Or There! Do not believe it. For false christs and false prophets will rise and show great signs and wonders to deceive, if possible, even the elect. See, I have told you beforehand.'" Matthew 24:22-25.

> "For thus says the Lord, 'When the seventy years are completed for Babylon …'" Jeremiah 29:10.

What a great passage of Scripture for us to lean into. Here we know the story. Daniel is probably reading his daily Scripture when he comes across these words. The Holy Spirit of revelation floods him, and he sees the season he is living in.

It is a chronological time, because it is an actual space of time, 70 years. Yes, the Lord can speak to us in chronological time. Yet, Israel was about to move, by the Holy Spirit of God, into a new season. Alleluia!

They were in a season of God's punishment for their rebellion, but Jehovah God, even in His mercy, had told them it would only be for 70 years, a generation. When the season they were living in had come to its fullness, God was ready to take them on a new walk with Him, a new level of knowing Him, a new Anointing in Him.

Even though they did not become a nation again in their land at that time, they were being led into their next step in God. God had NOT totally forsaken them. He was still working with them, leading them, guiding them, drawing them. He had His remnant and prophets who were still walking with Him and listening. God still had much to do before they could come back to their native land and become the nation of Israel again.

You can tell when there has been a shift and a change in the Spirit. You can tell when God is moving and doing something new. We may not always know what to expect, but His prophets do. Listen to the man of God, God has put in your life. He is being given instructions from the Holy Spirit. He has been given the responsibility to watch over you. God will speak to your heart through him and confirm what He's been sharing with you in private. Yes, the Holy Spirit will confirm the season you are living in, and He will confirm His leading to you.

There are personal seasons in our lives we walk through with God, as I have already shown you, but this is a word given to a whole race of people, a whole nation of people.

We, as the Body of Christ, what is the season we are walking through with God now?

We know we are definitely living in the last days, the days of the return of Jesus. The signs are everywhere. These are the days the great prophets of old dreamed of seeing. Hebrews 11:13-16, 32-10, 12:1-2 talks about these days.

These are the days of the great latter day rain, as revealed in Deuteronomy 11:14, Proverbs 16:15, and James 5:7.

I believe this is the time and the season of the great outpouring of the Holy Spirit, as written about in the Books of Zechariah 10:1, Joel 2:23-24, 28-32, and Acts 2:17-21.

I believe we are living in the season at the end of the ages when God is covering the whole Earth with His Spirit, just like the waters cover the sea. However, there is a process of getting to that season of time. The children of Israel and Christian believers of Jesus, over the span of time, have been through a lot of persecution that is beyond our understanding. Only to say, the devil hates you and wants to kill, steal and destroy the work of God in you and on the Earth. That is because the devil hates God and lost the battle when Jesus was raised from the dead. He knows his time is at hand to be sent to his place in hell.

Don't let the devil have the satisfaction of smudging your testimony or witness with his filth. Lean into the Anointing of the Holy Spirit, and trust His leading.

For God, in His mercy, has made a way for everyone to spend eternity with Him. He has made a way for everyone to really know Him and experience Him. His love, His peace, His joy; His purpose, His calling and His destiny are all for you. The Holy Spirit and His Anointing in a real relationship are here for you and anyone who wants Him.

But let's look at this Scripture again.

> "For thus says the Lord, 'When the seventy years are completed for Babylon, I will visit you and keep My good word (or My promise) to you, causing you to return to this place (or to return to My presence).'" Jeremiah 29:10. (Emphasis added.)

Wow! God is so awesome! What an encouragement to His people. Immediately, Daniel knows what to do. He seeks God in prayer and fasting. He presses into God with all he has.

This is exactly what we need to do. When God breathes on His Word and reveals Himself to us, we need to stay there in His presence and receive the fullness of what He is saying to our hearts. Listen for more throughout the day and the days to come. Grow in God. Don't set it on a shelf; that is for outside sources. The Holy Spirit is not an outside source. Take what the Holy Spirit of God gives you and run with it, study it, and give it your best. When He speaks, it is with purpose and destiny for your soul and your life.

> "I will visit you and keep My good word (or My promise) to you!" Jeremiah 29:10.

Why? Why would He want to visit you and keep His word, His promise to you? Is it something you did that was so special? Is it your special gifting or your special works that you've done?

Of course not! First of all, it has nothing to do with us and all to do with Him. God is good! He loves you, and He wants you to know Him. He wants you to know His leading and His presence in your life, but that only comes through the fellowship of His Holy Spirit and Anointing.

Secondly, but equally to the first point, God is not a man that He should lie. It has to do with Who God is and His Character.

Man is created equal to man. All of mankind are liars. But there is no one created equal to God. There is no one else like Him! He is the Only One True Living God! All of creation is here because of Him.

When He says He is going to do something, then by golly, He will do it. But! It's on His timetable, not ours. Because, not like us, He is perfect in all that He does. We have to trust in the fact that God is good, and He knows what He is doing.

So here is Daniel, who has been carried away with all of Jerusalem into exile in Babylon for 70 years. He's an old man now. He's reading from the Scriptures, and it says:

> "For thus says the Lord, 'When the 70 years are completed for Babylon, I will visit you and keep My good word (or My promise) to you, causing you to return to this place (or to return to My presence).

> "For I know the thoughts and plans that I have for you, says the Lord, They are thoughts and plans for welfare and peace and not for evil, to give you hope in your future, (or final outcome).

> "Then you will call upon Me, and you will come and pray to Me, and I will hear and heed you."

In other words, He will listen to you when you talk to Him. That's not so hard; all you have to do is talk to Him from your heart.

> "Then you will seek Me, and you will inquire for Me, and you will require Me as a vital necessity."

That is what He wants! He wants you to want Him! He wants you to come to the place that you need Him more than the air you breathe. Don't forget who we are talking about here, GOD!

> "'and then you will find Me when you search for Me with all your heart! I will be found by you,' says the Lord, 'and I will release you from captivity and gather you from all the nations and all the places to which I have driven you,' says the Lord, 'and I will bring you back to the place from which I caused you to be carried away captive.'" Jeremiah 29:10-14 (AMP).

So what do we need to do in order to guard our Anointing? We need to have an understanding of the valuable season of God's fullness of time we are living in. What you do is important! It makes it much easier to walk by faith when you know there is more to the picture than what meets the eye. God is big! And His ways are bigger than us. The Word says His ways are higher than ours, obviously.

We need to trust Him and know, "He is working all things together for good to those who love Him and are called to His purpose." Romans 8:28.

Eternity is not that far away.

Chapter 10

HOW TO
GUARD YOUR ANOINTING

ABSOLUTE THREE—BE FOCUSED!

Let me ask you a question. In the Scriptures, why does God call us His little children? How can He put all of us in the same category, when there are obviously Christians who are more mature than others? It's because we ALL have His calling, His purpose, and His destiny on our lives.

We are all running in the same race. What we do with our lives here determines the outcome of our eternity. How can I be so bold to say such a thing? It's because God is a rewarder of those who diligently seek Him.

When Jesus was faced with the reality of the cross, when that moment came, he was able to endure it because His focus was on the prize. His focus was on the souls of men and women being set free from death, hell and the grave through His obedient sacrifice.

Our focus should also be on the prize. Our prize is Jesus! One day, we will see Him face-to-Face. What a wonderful day that will be. On that day we will be laying our crowns of obedience at His feet. Serving Him with honor and respect is what we do, for He is the Author and the Finisher of our faith. Without Him there is no hope for anyone.

> "Therefore we also, since we are surrounded by so great a cloud of witnesses, let us lay aside every weight, and the sin which so easily ensnares us, and let us run with endurance the race that is set before us, looking unto Jesus, the author and finisher of our faith, WHO FOR THE JOY THAT WAS SET BEFORE HIM ENDURED THE CROSS, despising the shame, and has sat down at the right hand of the throne of God. For CONSIDER HIM WHO ENDURED SUCH HOSTILITY FROM SINNERS AGAINST HIMSELF, lest you become weary and discouraged in your souls." Hebrews 12:1-3.

What a courageous Champion our Savior is! He did it for us! He endured the cross! Let us always "consider" and remember that fact.

"Endure hardship with us like a good soldier of Christ Jesus. No one serving as a soldier gets involved in civilian affairs—he wants to please his commanding officer. Similarly, if anyone competes as an athlete, he does not receive the Victor's Crown unless he competes according to the rules." 2 Timothy 2:3-5 (NIV).

"Remember that in a race everyone runs, but only one person gets the prize. You must also run in such a way that you will win! All athletes practice strict self-control. They do it to win a prize that will fade away, but we do it for an eternal prize! So I run straight to the goal with purpose in every step. I am not like a boxer who misses his punches. I discipline my own body like an athlete, training it to do what it should. Otherwise, I fear that after preaching to others I myself might be disqualified." 1 Corinthians 9:24-27 (NLT).

Yes! It is possible to guard your Anointing, but you must remain focused on the prize. Run this race, and run it with diligence!

The Lord will reward you with more than you could possibly imagine.

> "No eye has seen, no ear has heard,
> And no mind has imagined
> What God has prepared
> For those who love Him!"
> 1 Corinthians 2:9 (NLT).

FROM THE AUTHOR

Hi! I am Judy Block, and I have been in love with Jesus for as long as I can remember. My first experience with Him was when I was about 4 years old. I cannot imagine walking though this life without the friendship of the King of Glory, Jesus. His direction and His faithfulness are overwhelming.

When I was 21, I received the baptism of the Holy Spirit. Now, over 30 years later, He has inspired me to write about His Anointing. The Holy Spirit and His Anointing is Someone I personally know. The vision I had at 2 a.m. gives us the key to the Anointing. The knowledge and personal experiences in this book are written in such a way as to help you know Him, grow in Him and challenge you to want more of the Anointing.

He said in His written Word, "Draw close to Me, and I will draw close to you." When you seek, look for, and entreat for Him with all your heart, you will find Him, and He will answer you. He is a rewarder of those who diligently seek Him. "Ask and you shall receive, seek and you shall find, knock and the door will be opened to you." If you will seek first the Kingdom of God and His righteousness, He will add all those things you have need of to you. So, delight yourself in the Lord, and He will give you the desires of your heart. For those who KNOW their God, those who are in relationship and friendship with their God, will do great exploits!

In other words, when you put the Lord first in your life, He will put you first!

Jesus said, "And unless those days were shortened, no flesh would be saved; but for the elect's sake those days will be shortened ... For false christs and false prophets will rise and show great signs and wonders to deceive, if possible, even the elect." (Matthew 24:22, 24).

Yes, the deception of the enemy is going to be great in these last days before His return, but Jesus has not left us without help, real Help, the Holy Spirit and His Anointing. It is the Holy Spirit who will lead us into all truth so we don't get led astray.

God has purpose, plans, callings, destinies and things in His heart just for you. With the personal indwelling help of the Holy Spirit and His Anointing it is possible for you to fulfill it all.

Thank you for picking up this book. I know you will not be disappointed.

For further information or to contact Judy, go to:
www.JudyBlockMinistries.org